WHEN I WAS A BOY

When I was a Boy can be yesterday or fifty years ago, depending on the age of the reader (and readers of any age will love this book). For Erich Kästner, the well-known children's author who admits to being born in 1899, it was only yesterday, because he believes that 'what we have forgotten is old. The unforgettable was yesterday.' So in this delightful book he recreates his own childhood, the last half-century vanishes, and Dresden, the lovely city in which the young Emil Erich grew up, exists beyond the rubble which is all that is left today. A whole host of Kästner relations exist too: but above them all stands Frau Ida Amalia Kästner, the mother to out-mother all mothers, whose aim in life was to become the best mother in the world and who achieved it because she was as incapable of failure as she was of going downhill on a bicycle.

Oddly enough Frau Kästner was a hairdresser, and those who remember Frau Tischbein in *Emil and the Detectives* may wonder if they have not here stumbled upon her prototype. And Frau Tischbein is not the only one; there are many other characters in Erich Kästner's well-loved books whose antecedents are clearly traceable in *When I was a Boy*. It is not often that we have such a chance to go behind the scenes, as it were, and see how some of the most famous of all children's books came to be written.

ALSO BY ERICH KÄSTNER

ERICH KÄSTNER

WHEN I

WAS

A BOY

TRANSLATED FROM THE GERMAN
BY ISABEL AND FLORENCE MCHUGH
ILLUSTRATED BY HORST LEMKE

FRANKLIN WATTS, INC.
575 Lexington Ave., New York 22

CONTENTS

NO BOOK
WITHOUT A
FOREWORD

DEAR Children and Non-Children:

My friends have, for a long time past, laughed at me because none of my books ever appears without a preface. Indeed, some of them have actually been published with two and even three prefaces. In this respect I am quite tireless. And even if it is a bad habit I shall never be able to overcome it; first of all, because there's nothing harder to overcome than a bad habit, and second, because I don't consider it a bad habit at all.

A preface to a book is just as important and attractive as a garden in front of a house. Naturally, there are houses without little front gardens, and books without any sort of introduction, preface or foreword. But I prefer books with a front garden — sorry, I mean a foreword. I don't like to have visitors falling into the house as the door opens. It isn't good for the visitors, nor for the house — nor even for the door.

A front garden with flower beds, of many-coloured pansies, for instance, and a little path leading up to the house, and three or four steps up to the door and the bell — is that really a bad thing? Huge blocks of flats, and even sky-scrapers seventy storeys high, have become necessary in the course of time; and big books as heavy as bricks have, too. All the same, my preference is still for cosy little houses with pansies and dahlias in the front gardens; and slim manageable volumes with a foreword.

Perhaps that is because I grew up in big tenement houses that had no gardens at all. The backyard was my front garden, and the pole on which carpets were beaten was my lime tree. Not that that is anything to cry about, nor ever was. Backyards and carpet poles have a lot to be said for them; and I cried very little and laughed a great deal. It is only that lilac bushes and elder bushes are beautiful in an altogether different and lovelier way. I knew that even when I was a little boy, and now I know it still better. Because now at last I have a little front garden of my own, and behind the house there is a meadow. And there are roses and violets, tulips, snowdrops, narcissi, crowsfoot, lobelia, forget-me-nots, bluebells, and great flowering grasses a yard high caressed by the summer winds. And I also have black alder and lilac bushes, and two tall ash trees, and an old gnarled elder. And there are bluetits, great tits, linnets, nuthatches, bullfinches, blackbirds, spotted woodpeckers and magpies. Sometimes I could almost envy myself!

In this book I want to tell children something of my own childhood – something, not everything. Otherwise this would become one of those great tomes heavy as bricks which I dislike so much; and anyway, my desk is not a brickyard. Besides, not everything that children experience is suitable for other children to read about. That may sound a trifle odd, but it is true. You may take my word for it!

It is now fifty years since I was a little boy; and fifty years, after all, are half a century. (I hope I haven't miscalculated.) And one fine day I thought to myself that it might interest you to know

how a little boy lived half a century ago. (I hope I haven't miscalculated that either!)

So many things in those days were different from what they are today. I travelled in horse trams. Even then the tram ran on tram-lines, but it was drawn by a horse, and the conductor was also the driver and cracked a whip. Just when people had got used to the electric tram the fashion for hobble-skirts came in, and ladies took to wearing very long tight skirts. They could take only tiny little steps, and they couldn't climb on to the trams at all. They had to be heaved on to the platform by the conductors and other strong men, amid laughter; at the same time they had to tilt their heads to one side because they wore hats as big as cart-wheels with enormous feathers and hatpins half a yard long, on which the police compelled them to wear guards.

In those days we still had a Kaiser in Germany. He wore big moustaches curled up at the ends, and his Berlin court hairdresser used to advertise in the newspapers and magazines the particular kind of moustache-binder which the Kaiser favoured. The result was that every morning German gentlemen put a big wide moustache-binder over their mouths after shaving, looked very silly, and couldn't speak at all for half an hour.

We also had a King of Saxony. Every year imperial manœuvres took place in honour of the Kaiser, and on the King's birthday there was a royal parade. The uniforms of the guards and riflemen, and especially those of the cavalry regiments, were gloriously colourful. And when the household cavalry with their gleaming helmets and breastplates, the hussars with their laced tunics and brown fur caps, the uhlans with their ulankas and shakos, and the mounted riflemen, all perched high on horseback, with sabres drawn and lances erect, trotted past the Royal Stand on the Alaunplatz in Dresden, the excitement was tremendous and everyone yelled hurrah. The trumpets blared, the harness bells tinkled, and the drummers beat their kettle-drums until the air thundered. Those parades were far and away the most lavish and magnificent revues and operettas I have ever seen in my life.

The monarch whose birthday was celebrated with so much colour and noise was called Friedrich August. He was the last King of Saxony but he did not know it at the time. He often drove through the royal residence city with his children. His bodyguard sat beside the coachman with arms folded, wearing a shimmering feather hat. And the little princes and princesses waved at us other children from the open carriage. The King waved too, and smiled kindly at us. And we waved back and felt a little sorry for him, because we and all the world knew that his

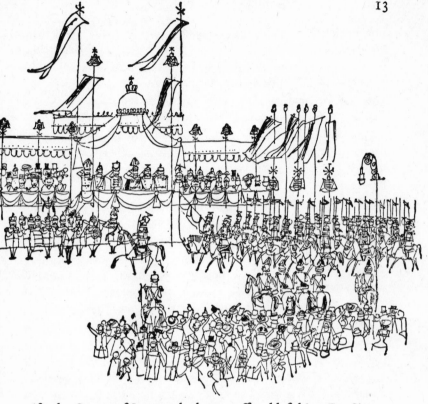

wife, the Queen of Saxony, had gone off and left him. For Signor Toselli, an Italian violinist! So the poor King had become a rather pathetic figure, and the little princes and princesses no longer had a mother.

Towards Christmas he often walked along the gaily lit Prager Strasse all alone in the evening, wearing a high-collared military coat like that worn by officers, and stood gazing thoughtfully at the glittering shop windows. Children's clothes and toys were the things that seemed to interest him most. It was snowing. The Christmas trees twinkled in the shop windows. The passers-by nudged each other, whispered, 'The King!' and hurried on so as not to disturb him. He was lonely; he loved his children; and that was why the people loved him. If he had gone into Rarisch the butcher's and said to one of the girls, 'A couple of hot frankfurters with plenty of mustard, for eating here,' she would definitely not have curtsied, and it's quite certain she would not have said, 'We are greatly honoured, Your Majesty.' She would just have asked, 'With or without rolls?' And we others, including my mother and myself, would have looked the other way so as not to spoil his appetite. But he probably didn't trust himself that far. Anyhow, he didn't go into Rarisch's but just walked along the See Strasse, stopped before Lehmann & Leichsenrings, a beautiful delicatessen shop, passed along the Altmarkt, strolled down the Schloss Strasse and inspected the tin soldiers drawn up in battle formation in Zeuner's window, and then his Christmas stroll was over. On the other side of the street stood his castle, where his approach had been noted. The Guard paraded and words of command rang out. The soldiers presented arms, and with a casual salute the last King of Saxony disappeared into his house, which was far too big for him.

Yes, half a century is a long time. But I often think it was only yesterday. Such a lot of things have happened in between: wars and electric light, revolutions and inflation, dirigible airships and the League of Nations; the deciphering of the Babylonian cuneiform script, and aeroplanes that fly faster than sound. But the seasons and the school lessons went on just the same then, and they are still going on today. Almost everything has changed, and almost everything has remained the same.

Was it only yesterday or was it really half a century ago that I used to do my home-work under the smoky paraffin lamp, and its glass chimney would crack suddenly with a thin little click and have to be changed cautiously with the pot-cloth? Nowadays electric fuses go pop, and we have to strike a match and hunt round for a new bit of fuse wire, and screw it in. Is there all that difference? Well, yes, the light is brighter today than it was then. And you don't have to carry home the electric current in a paraffin can. A lot of things have become more convenient. But have they become nicer? I really don't know. Perhaps they have, and perhaps they haven't.

When I was a little boy I used to trot off to the Co-operative Stores in Grenadier Strasse in the morning before going to school. 'A litre and a half of paraffin and a fresh four-pound loaf, second quality,' I would say to the shop-girl. Then I would run on with the change, the discount discs, the bread and the splashing can. The snowflakes danced round the flickering gas street-lamps. The frost sewed my nostrils together with fine stitches. Next I would go to Kiessling the butcher's. 'A quarter of a pound of home-made black pudding and liver sausage, half and half.' And now to Frau Kletsch the greengrocer. 'A lump of butter and six pounds of potatoes, and please Mother said to tell you the last were frozen.' And then home with the bread, paraffin, sausage, butter and potatoes. My breath puffed white from my mouth like the smoke of a steamer on the Elbe. The warm four-pound loaf under my arm kept slipping down. The money rattled in my pocket. The paraffin splashed about in the can. The net bag of potatoes banged against my knee as I ran. The front door screeched on its hinges. Then up the stairs three steps àt a time to the third floor, and no hand free to ring the bell. I would push the door with my foot and it would open. 'Can't you ring?' Mother would ask. 'No, Mamma, what with?' And she would laugh. 'Have you forgotten anything?' 'No fear!' 'Very well, come on, young man!' And there at the table she would give me a cup of malted coffee with Karlsbad fig juice in it, and a big side of the warm loaf – the 'kissing crust', with fresh butter, while my school satchel would be waiting packed on the landing, as though it were hopping impatiently from one leg to the other.

★

'More than fifty years have passed since then,' declares the calendar, that horny old book-keeper in the office of history, who controls chronology and with ink and ruler marks the leap years in blue and draws a red line at the beginning of each century. 'No!' cries memory, shaking her curly locks. 'It was only yesterday. Or at most the day before,' she adds softly with a little laugh. Which of them is wrong?

They are both right, for there are two kinds of time. The one kind can be measured with instruments and calculations, just like streets or plots of ground. But the other chronology, our memory, has nothing to do with metres and months, decades or acres. What we have forgotten is old. The unforgettable was yesterday. The measure here is not the time but the value. And the most precious of all things, whether happy or sad, is our childhood. Do not forget the unforgettable. I believe that this advice cannot be given early enough.

With it my foreword ends. And on the next page the first chapter begins. That is as it should be. For if the axiom 'No book without a foreword' has a certain justification, the converse is still more true. And it is:

NO FOREWORD WITHOUT A BOOK

I

THE KÄSTNERS AND THE AUGUSTINS

WHEN someone sets out to tell about himself he generally begins by telling about other people altogether. People he has never seen and never could have seen. People he has never met and never will meet. People who are dead long ago and whom he knows next to nothing about. When someone sets out to tell about himself, he generally begins with his ancestors.

That is understandable, because without ancestors one would be quite alone on the ocean of time, like a castaway on a tiny uninhabited island. Quite alone. Every mother's son of us. Every grandmother's son of us. Every great-great-grandmother's son of us. Through our ancestors we are closely related and linked down the centuries with the past, both by blood and marriage. And one day we ourselves shall be ancestors; ancestors of people who are not yet born and yet are already related to us.

In former times the Chinese used to erect altars to their ancestors in their houses, and they used to kneel down before those altars and meditate on this relationship to their ancestors. The emperor and the mandarin, the merchant and the coolie would each meditate on the fact that he was not only the emperor or the coolie but also the individual link in an unbreakable chain, and that he would continue to be this even when he was dead. Whether the chain

17

was of gold, of pearls, or only of glass, whether his ancestors were Sons of Heaven, knights, or only doorkeepers, no one was alone. None was so proud or so poor as to be that.

But we don't want to get solemn about it. Whether we like it or not, we are not Chinese. So I will not erect a house altar to my ancestors. I will tell you a little about them instead.

To tell you 'a little' about my father's ancestors is quite easy, because I know nothing, or next to nothing, about them. Their names and the dates of their births, marriages and deaths were conscientiously entered in church registers by various Protestant pastors throughout Saxony. The men were craftsmen, had many children, and outlived their wives, who generally died in child-birth. And many of the newborn babies died with their mothers. That was the way, not only with the Kästners but all over Europe and America. And it went on like that until Doctor Ignaz Philipp Semmelweiss found out how to prevent childbed fever. That was about a hundred years ago. Doctor Semmelweiss has been called 'The Saviour of the Mothers'; and people have been so busy praising him that they have forgotten to erect any monuments to his memory. But that doesn't belong here!

My father's father, Christian Gottlieb Kästner, was a joiner and lived in Penig, a little Saxon town on the river Mulde. He and his wife Laura, née Eidam, had eleven children, five of whom died in infancy. Two of his sons became joiners like their father. Another, Uncle Karl, became a blacksmith. And Emil Kästner, my father, learned the trade of saddler.

Perhaps it was from them and their forebears that I have in-herited the careful craftsmanship which I apply to my calling. And perhaps I owe my talent for gymnastics, which I admit has gone a bit rusty now, to my Uncle Hermann who, at seventy-five, was still head of the older men's team in the Penig Gymnastics Society. But it is quite certain that the Kästners have handed me on one family characteristic which always surprises and often annoys my friends – a chronic aversion to travel.

We Kästners have no particular curiosity to see the great world. We suffer, not from love of roving, but from love of home. Why should we go to the Black Forest, or climb Mount Everest, or see Trafalgar Square? The chestnut tree in front of the house, the Wolfshügel hill which overlooks Dresden, or the Altmarkt, do us quite well. If we could take our beds and our living-room windows with us, we might perhaps be induced to budge. But as for going off to foreign parts and leaving our home at home. No, thank you! There is not a mountain so high, an oasis so mysterious, a harbour so exciting, a Niagara Falls so loud that we feel we must go and see them. It might be all right if we could go to sleep at home and wake up in Buenos Aires, for instance. The being there would probably be tolerable for a while; but what about the getting there? We would never do it. I'm afraid we're far too set in our ways and fond of our comfort for that. But to offset these doubtful qualities we Kästners have one virtue: we're utterly incapable of being bored. A ladybird on the window-pane can absorb our attention completely. It doesn't have to be a lion in the jungle.

All the same, my ancestors, and even my father, travelled at least once in their lives – on Shanks's pony, as journeymen artisans, with their journeyman's letter in their pockets. But they did not do so by choice. Their trade guilds required it of them. A man who had not worked in other towns and under strange masters was not allowed to qualify as a master himself. One had to serve as a journeyman artisan away if one wanted to be a master of one's trade at home; and this the Kästners definitely wanted to be, whether they were joiners, blacksmiths, tailors, stove-fitters or saddlers. Generally, however, this journeyman's tramp remained their first and last journey. Once they became masters their travelling days were over.

When my father got out of a Dresden taxi in front of my house in Munich last August – a bit plaintive and tired, for after all he's ninety – he had come only to see how I live and to look out at the lawn from my window. Except for his concern for me, wild horses would not have dragged him from his Dresden window. He, too, has a bit of green to look out at; and there are tits, chaffinches, blackbirds and magpies there as well, and many more sparrows than in Bavaria. So why should he take a journey except to see me?

I myself have seen a little more of the world than he and our ancestors. I have been in Copenhagen and Stockholm, Moscow and Leningrad, Paris and London, Vienna and Geneva, Edinburgh and Nice, Prague and Venice, Dublin and Amsterdam, Radebeul and Lugano, Belfast and Garmisch-Partenkirchen. But I don't like travelling. Unfortunately, however, it is much the same in my trade too – a man must go away from home if he wants to be a master one fine day at home. And I too would very much like to become a master of my craft. But that's beside the point!

My mother, Ida Amalia Kästner, came of a Saxon family named Augustin. In the sixteenth century these ancestors of mine were called Augsten and Augstin and Augusten. The spelling Augustin only appears from about 1650 onwards in the parish church registers, and in the treasurer's accounts of the town of Döbeln.

How do I know that? Because there is a 'Chronicle of the Augustin Family' which goes back to the year 1568. That was an interesting year. In that year Elizabeth I of England threw Mary Queen of Scots into prison, and King Philip II of Spain did the same to his son Don Carlos. The Duke of Alba executed the two Counts Egmont and Horn in Brussels. Pieter Brueghel painted his picture, 'The Peasant Wedding'. And my ancestor Hans Augustin was fined by the Town Council of Döbeln for baking loaves which were under weight. Solely thanks to this fine he got into the annual accounts of the town and so into written history, together with Mary Queen of Scots, Don Carlos, Count Egmont and Pieter Brueghel. If he had not been caught out that time we would know nothing at all about him. Or at least not until 1577; for in that year again he was fined for selling underweight rolls and loaves, and the fine was once more entered in the books. The same thing happened in 1578, 1580 and, for the last time, in the year 1605. So in order to become famous one must bake loaves which are too small, and be caught out. Or else loaves which are too big; but no baker has done that yet, at least I have never heard or read of one.

Hans Augustin's son Caspar is called Caspar I in my chronicle. He was a baker too and is mentioned in the annals of Döbeln three times – in 1613, 1621 and 1629. Can you guess why? Caspar I also baked loaves which were too small! Yes, indeed, the Augustins were a tough lot. But this did not get them far on in the world, although they bought barns, gardens and fields, cultivated hops, and not only baked bread but also brewed beer. First the plague descended on the town and carried off half the clan. In 1636 the Croats and in 1645 the Swedes plundered the little Saxon town. For of course the Thirty Years War was on then, and the soldiers slaughtered the cattle, used the crops as fodder for their beasts, loaded up the beds and copper bakehouse utensils on Caspar Augustin's carts, and burned what they could not take away with them. Then off they went with their booty to do the same in the next little town.

Caspar Augustin's son was also called Caspar, so the chronicle calls him Caspar II. He was a baker also, was head of the family until 1652, and worried himself into his grave. For his brother Johann, who lived in Danzig, had turned up when the war was over and demanded his share of the inheritance, which of course the Swedes had carried off to Sweden with them. He had not cared to travel and so claim his inheritance while the war was on,

but now he had the audacity to demand heavy interest for it. There was a lawsuit which ended in a settlement, and the whole matter was recorded neatly and precisely by the town clerk. And in this way my ancestors got their names into history once more, this time through a family quarrel and not on account of under-sized loaves. So you see even a quarrel between brothers can make people famous.

I can see that I shall have to be a bit more brief if I am ever to get to the real subject of this book — namely, myself. Very well, then, I shall be brief. What important things have I still got to tell? Well, the Augustins got on their feet again, and every one of them, whether his name was Wolfgang Augustin, Johann Georg I, Johann Georg II or Johann Georg III — every single one of them became a master baker. In 1730 the town of Döbeln was burned down. Then, just when it was recovering from that, there was the Seven Years War and the Prussians came. They made the town one of their winter quarters, for in those days wars took long holidays in the winter. Even Frederick the Great could not change that. So the regiments settled in comfortably and instead of destroying the enemy towns and villages with powder and shot, they literally ate the inhabitants out of house and home. When the inhabitants had more or less got over this, along came Napoleon with his Grand Army, and by the time he was beaten at the Battle of Leipzig the Augustins too were down and out once more. This was first because Döbeln is near Leipzig, and secondly because the King of Saxony had been an ally of Napoleon. He was on the losing side, and his subjects, including the inhabitants of Döbeln, suffered for this even more than he did himself.

But the Augustins did not remain down. They became fairly prosperous once more. Again they were bakers, and again they were licensed to brew and sell beer. By this time they had already been bakers for three hundred years, in spite of plagues and fires and wars. Then, in the year 1847, came the great decisive change: the baker Johann Carl Friedrich Augustin started a cartage and livery stable business. From that historic date onwards my mother's forebears dealt in horses; and it is certainly not their fault that that magnificent animal, the horse, is dying out, and with it the trades of carter, livery stabler and horsedealer.

The third child of Johann Carl Friedrich Augustin was baptized Carl Friedrich Louis. He became a blacksmith and horsedealer in Kleinpelsen near Döbeln; and seven of his sons became horsedealers. Two of them actually became millionaires.[1] More money can be earned by dealing in horses than by making loaves and rolls, even if you make them under weight. Besides you can love

[1] A millionaire in German marks is not nearly so rich as an English millionaire, or even as an American one. In those days he was a man who amassed a fortune of some £30,000 or thereabouts. — *Translator's Note.*

horses even if you buy and sell them and earn money by them. With bread, that is much, much harder. At last the Augustins had found their true vocation.

The blacksmith of Kleinpelsen was my grandfather. His horse-dealer sons were my uncles. And his daughter Ida Amalia was my mother. But she doesn't come in here. For my mother must have a quite separate chapter all to herself.

2

LITTLE IDA AND HER BROTHERS

M Y mother was born on April 9th, 1871, in the village of Kleinpelsen. And, as so often happens, there was a war on then – the
Franco-Prussian War. For that reason her birthplace did not become nearly as famous as did Wilhelmshöhe near Cassel in the
same year when Napoleon III, Emperor of the French, was
imprisoned there; or as Versailles near Paris, where King William
of Prussia was proclaimed Emperor of Germany.

The Emperor of the French was imprisoned in a German castle
and the German Emperor was proclaimed in a French castle. It
would have been much simpler and certainly much cheaper the
other way round. But world history can never cost enough. If a
grocer did as many stupid things and made as many mistakes in
his little shop as the statesmen and generals make in their great
countries, he would be bankrupt within a month. And instead of
figuring in the golden book of history, he would appear on the
Official Receiver's list. But that, again, is beside the point!

Little Ida Augustin, my future mamma, spent her childhood
in a farmhouse. This home of hers had all sorts of things – a big
barn, a front garden with pansies and asters, a dozen brothers and
sisters, a farmyard full of fowls, an old orchard full of cherry and
plum trees, a stable, a lot of work, and a long way to school. For

the school was in a neighbouring village. And there was not much to be learned in that school, because it had only one teacher and two classes; one for the children from seven to ten, and the other for the children from eleven to confirmation. There was simply nothing to be learned in that school except reading, writing and arithmetic; and this was fearfully tedious for clever children. Four years in the same class! That would bore anyone to tears.

In those days it was hotter in the summer and colder in the winter than it is nowadays, I don't know why. There are people who say they do, but I have a suspicion they are only pretending.

In winter the snow sometimes piled up so high that the front door wouldn't open. The children had to climb out of the window if they wanted to go to school; or rather, because my grandfather thought they ought to want to go. In order to open the door in spite of the snow a tunnel had first to be dug, and the children crawled through this into the open. That was quite good fun, but it did not last long, because outside an icy wind blew over the fields. The children sank up to their thighs in the snow, and their fingers and toes and ears hurt so much from the cold that tears came to their eyes. And when they finally arrived at the school, drenched through, half frozen and late, there was nothing really sensible and interesting for them to learn.

All this did not discourage little Ida in the least. She climbed out through the window. She crawled through the snow tunnel. She froze and cried on the way to school. But this did not worry her, for she was hungry and thirsty for knowledge. She was determined to learn everything that the old teacher knew himself. And though he did not know much, he certainly knew more than little Ida.

Her elder brothers, especially Franz, Robert and Paul, had absolutely different ideas about school. They considered sitting in a classroom a waste of time. The little knowledge of reading and writing they would need later on was quickly learned. And as for arithmetic! I believe those three boys could reckon in their cradles, even before they could say the words 'Mother' and 'Father'. Arithmetic was just born in them, like breathing, hearing and seeing.

For this reason the journey to school was a means of getting away from home, but quite often they finished up somewhere other than at school. Where did the little fellows spend their time, and what were they up to? Playing ball on some distant field? Or breaking window-panes? Or teasing some bad-tempered

watch-dog to make it pull at its chain? Of course they didn't exactly avoid doing these things, but generally they were doing only one thing when they should have been in the village school. They were trading in rabbits.

Even at that age they would have much preferred trading in horses; but horses are formidable animals, and far too big to be hidden away in wooden boxes. Besides, rabbits multiply, as we know, 'like rabbits'. They keep on having baby rabbits. You only have to find a few turnips and carrots and heads of lettuce, and the dear little creatures thrive exceedingly and produce splendid offspring.

Well, the three brothers found their rabbit fodder, and I can wager they never paid for it. If you produce cheaply you can sell cheaply. Business flourished. The Brothers Augustin provided Kleinpelsen and district so steadily and so abundantly with rabbits that the fame of the firm reached the ears of my grandfather. He was not nearly as proud of his sons as might have been expected, and when they would not own up, even after a thorough good hiding which left his arms aching, he turned to little Ida and questioned her. She told him what she knew, and that was a whole lot.

Robert, Franz and Paul did not like this at all, so they took their sister away and had a little talk with her on the quiet. For quite a time afterwards she had blue marks which turned first green and then yellow before they finally disappeared.

But apart from the blue marks the talk was pretty futile. Almost like an international conference. Their sister explained that Father had wanted to know the truth, and a person had to tell the truth under any circumstances; you were taught that both at home and at school. But the three brothers had spent far too little time either at home or at school to share this view. They said Ida had blabbed and was neither a good comrade nor a good sister, and she ought to be ashamed of herself.

Which of them was right? It is hard to say. The problem is older than the whole Augustin clan. It is as old as the world itself. Should you lie to your parents for the sake of your brothers and sisters? Or must you split on your brothers and sisters in obedience to your parents?

If Grandfather had kept a sharper eye on his young scamps he would not have had to question little Ida. But he was often away from home, buying or selling a horse. Was that his fault?

If the three young rascals had been well behaved and exemplary youths, little Ida would not have had to tell on them. But the business instinct was in their blood. Their father traded in horses. They, instead of going to school, traded in rabbits. Was that their fault?

The only person who suffered any pangs of conscience over the matter was little Ida. And why? She went to school like a good child. She helped nobly with the housework. She looked after her younger brothers and sisters. And when she was questioned, she told the truth. Was that her fault?

Dear children, please don't skip these lines. Perhaps their theme is not as interesting as the Franco-Prussian War of 1870-1, or the illicit rabbit trade; but it is more important than both of them together. Therefore I will repeat the three points once more.

First point: a father who is so busy earning enough money for his family that he has not time to supervise them properly, catches three of his twelve children doing something wrong, wallops them, and feels that with this all is well once more as far as he is concerned. Second point: three boys play truant from school, get a hiding from their father, thrash their sister, and feel that all is well as far as they are concerned. And the third point: a little girl, good and honest to the core, who loves her parents and brothers and sisters, is asked to tell the truth, and tells it. And thereupon everything goes wrong as far as she is concerned.

That's how it was, and it was tragic. My mother suffered her whole life long – and she lived to be over eighty – for having told the truth that time, when she was little Ida. Was it treachery on her part? Should she have lied? Why did her father have to ask her of all people? She tortured herself with question after question, and never found a satisfactory answer.

Many, many years later, long after the little rabbit-dealer Franz had become the wealthy horsedealer Augustin, with his beautiful villa and his motor-car and chauffeur, it was still evident that he had by no means forgotten the incident. Nor indeed had my mother. And when we visited him at Christmas and were sitting peacefully under the Christmas tree, drinking mulled wine and eating raisin buns — but that doesn't belong here either!

Life went on its way in Kleinpelsen. My mother's mother died. A stepmother came into the house, bore the blacksmith and horsedealer Carl Friedrich Louis Augustin three children and loved the children of the first marriage just as dearly as her own. She was a kind, noble-hearted woman. I remember her myself. Her daughter Alma, my mother's half-sister, had a tobacco shop in the Bahnhof Strasse in Döbeln when I was a little boy.

Every time the door-bell rang the tall white-haired old lady got up from her armchair and walked with grave dignity into the shop to serve the customers. A packet of Bremen shag, five miniature cigars for tenpence, a roll of chewing tobacco, a packet of ten cigarettes. The shop had a delightful smell, and the old woman beside whom I used to stand behind the counter, was a lady. If the Empress Maria Theresa had sold chewing tobacco in Döbeln she would have looked just like Aunt Alma's old mother. But that doesn't belong here.

For we are still in Kleinpelsen. The elder brothers and sisters of little Ida, who was meantime growing up herself too, had left school. And they had also left home. Lina and Emma went 'in service', as it was called. They became servant-maids and very capable ones too, for of course they had been taught very thoroughly how to work at home.

And what about the brothers, the secret firm of rabbit-dealers, who had been unmasked? What did they learn? Horsedealing? For this they would have needed two things — knowledge of horses, and what is called capital. As for knowledge of horses, they had that right enough for they had grown up in the stables as other children grow up in the kindergarten or the church choir. But their father,

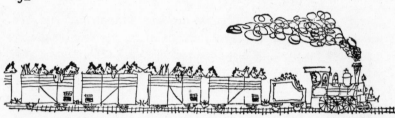

my grandfather, had not the money they would have required. When he bought or sold a horse it was a great event for himself and his family, and if a horse he had on hand died of glanders or colic it was a catastrophe.

What would my grandfather have said if anyone had told him then that his sons Robert and Franz would one day buy a hundred, perhaps two hundred, horses on a single visit to one of the great Continental horse fairs in Schleswig-Holstein, Denmark, Belgium or Holland? That whole train-loads of stamping horses would roll towards Dresden and Döbeln, to the stables of the famous firm of Augustin? That the colonels of the cavalry regiments and the managers of the breweries would fall over each other in their excitement when Robert in Döbeln and Franz in Dresden paraded their new consignments of horses for sale?

If anyone had told my grandfather that in those days he would have roared with laughter in spite of the asthma that was beginning to plague him. He would not have believed a word of it. Nor would he have believed that those same sons would almost forget him when he was poor and sick to death and they already wealthy. But that does not come in here, not yet anyway.

He had them taught the trade of butcher, and they were pleased with it. Their ancestors had been bakers for three hundred years. Now their descendants became butchers. And why not? Cattle and pigs are not horses, to be sure, but they are quadrupeds, and that's something. And if a man kills sheep and pigs and cattle long enough, and turns them into cutlets and liver sausage and so on, one day he may be able to buy a horse. A fine big live horse, and the straw and oats it needs.

And after he has bought the first horse cheap, fed it up, groomed it, tended it and sold it at a profit, it is easier to buy two horses, and after waiting shrewdly for the chance to sell well, invest the profit again in more horses. Luck, astuteness and industry all combined. Three horses, four horses, five horses, stabled at first in other people's stalls. Then the first stable of his own in some backyard. His own horses, his own mangers, his own bridles and halters.

And still carrying on the butcher's shop. Five o'clock in the morning at the slaughtering yard; then to the cold store; then to the slaughter-house to make fresh sausages and saveloys and lay

down fresh pork in pickle; then into the shop with snow-white apron and carefully parted and brilliantined hair, smiling at the lady customers and slyly laying a thumb on the scales when weighing out to them. Then to the horses in the stables; then into a pub with the lessee of a factory canteen to secure an order; then off to bargain for a cheap lot of oats and to sell a six-year-old horse as a three-year-old; then to weigh out ten lots of garlic sausage; back behind the counter again, at the chopping-block; and after the shop is closed, the counting of the day's takings; then to the stables again; once more into an inn, this time to 'soft-soap' the foreman of a furniture remover's; and finally to bed, to dream of reckoning up, and buying horses; and at five o'clock in the morning back in the slaughtering yard, and then to the cold store again. And on and on like that for years, half killing himself with work. And Augustin's young wife didn't have a much better time. She had nothing to do with the horses, of course, but she had to stand smiling in the butcher's shop from morning till evening and bear and rear two or three children into the bargain.

Then one fine day the butcher's shop was let or sold, and now the horsedealing got going in real earnest.

Three of my mother's brothers, the three former rabbit-dealers, Robert, Franz and Paul, became horsedealers in this way. But Paul specialized in carriage horses and riding-hacks, and he himself used to drive a dogcart through the streets of Dresden, looking as grand as a count. But Robert and Franz were made of sturdier stuff and got on much better than he did.

The other brothers, Bruno, Reinhold, Arno and Hugo, tried to do the same. They too began as butchers, and they got as far as two or three horses each. But then their luck forsook them; or perhaps it was their strength or their courage. Anyhow, they did not make the grade.

Reinhold died in the prime of life. Arno became an innkeeper.

Bruno helped his brother Franz as business manager. He got a kick from a horse on the jaw, and another on the leg. So he used to limp about the stables, shouted at by his brother the boss, while he himself shouted at the stablemen. And Hugo, my favourite uncle, remained a butcher to the end of his life after several extremely unsuccessful excursions into the land of horses.

His sons are butchers. His daughters have married butchers. They all love horses. But horses are dying out and so the Augustins' knowledge of horses is not going to help them any more. And they show no desire at all to deal in the horse's successor, the motor-car. For motor-cars are not alive; they only pretend to be.

When he was a young fellow my nephew Manfred tried something new. He became a professional wrestler. After all, a wrestler has to do with live things. Not with cattle or horses, yet with creatures that are alive. However, he did not really like wrestling, not as a permanent calling anyhow, though he was not at all a bad wrestler. I saw him performing several times at Krone's Stadium in Munich. He seemed very popular with the audience, especially the ladies, even when he was thrown now and then when his opponent got a grip on his throat or caught him in a scissor grip with his legs. For after all, it's a lot easier to carry half a calf out of the slaughter-house, across the yard and into the shop, than to fell 'The Steer of the Pampas', with his twenty-three-stone weight, when you yourself weigh a mere fourteen stone!

Anyhow, Manfred too has since qualified as a master-butcher. Sometime when I have a lot of leisure I'll count up all the butchers I have in my family. There are dozens of them. And out of all the butchers, blacksmiths and horsedealers, one solitary member of the clan, little Erich, the only child of little Ida, has become — of all things — a writer!

And they're all a trifle surprised at it, and they keep on being surprised whenever we meet and sit down for a chat. And I'm a bit surprised too, as a matter of fact, not at them but at myself. For even if I know a bit more than the average non-butcher about sausages and loins of veal, and have some knowledge of horses too, it always seems to me that I'm still only a step-Augustin.

But when you come to think of it, hasn't writing books also got to do with living creatures? For doesn't it amount to making a living out of life itself — working it up into mince or pressed ham? But that, dear reader, is definitely beside the point!

3

MY FUTURE PARENTS MEET AT LAST

WHEN little Ida had grown into a pretty young girl of sixteen she went in service too, for her younger sisters, Martha and Alma, were old enough now to help their mother. Compared with former days the house seemed almost empty. Ida left only her parents and five brothers and sisters behind. And new babies had stopped arriving by then.

She became a housemaid in a manor-house near Leisnig, where she served at table, ironed the fine underwear, helped in the kitchen and embroidered monograms on handkerchiefs and table-linen. She liked her job and her employers liked her. But one fine evening the owner of the manor, a gay cavalry officer, found he liked her rather too much and started making advances. Terrified, she bolted instantly out of the house, and ran in the dark through the gloomy forest and over the stubble-fields, until she arrived home, crying and exhausted, right in the middle of the night. The next day my grandfather went to the manor-house with his horse and cart and fetched away his daughter's chip basket. The dashing officer kept out of the way, luckily for himself.

After a time Ida found another job, this time in Döbeln, as nurse-companion to a lame old lady. There were no cavalry officers, who might have liked her too much, in the vicinity.

But her elder sisters, Lina and Emma, were there. They had married meanwhile, and both lived in Döbeln, in the same house, the Niedermühle. This was a real mill-house with a big water-wheel and a wooden mill-weir. The miller ground the wheat and rye which the farmers brought him into white flour, and they took it away in hundredweight sacks and sold it to the bakers and shopkeepers round about.

Aunt Lina had married a cousin of hers who had a cartage business, and so her name was Augustin after marriage as before. Aunt Emma, who lived in the flat above her, was now called Emma Hanns, and her husband dealt in fruit. He rented the endless avenues of plum and cherry trees which ran from one village to another over the surrounding countryside. And when the trees bent under the weight of ripe plums and cherries he hired a lot of men and women to pick them. The fruit used to be brought to Döbeln market in big wicker baskets and sold there. Some years the harvest was good, other years it was bad. Heat, rain and hailstone were Uncle's enemies, and quite often the proceeds of the harvest did not even cover the rent of the trees. When this happened Uncle Hanns had to borrow money, and he spent some of it in the taverns trying to drown his worries in beer.

At these times Aunt Emma came down to Aunt Lina to lament over her grievances. As the cartage business was none too flourishing either, Aunt Lina joined her plaint to hers and they made a duet of it, and the toddlers, who were crawling about the living-room, needed no encouragement to join in for all they were worth. And when my future mother, Ida, happened to be visiting and heard the dismal concert, she thought her own thoughts about it. And she thought them on the way back to the house of the lame old lady, to whom she had to read trashy novels until late into the night. Many a time she fell asleep from sheer exhaustion and only woke up, scared stiff, when the cross old

lady hammered on the floor with her stick and started rating her negligent companion-help.

What choice had a pretty but poor young girl in those days? To run away from amorous officers? To read silly books aloud to lame old ladies and fall asleep over them? Or to marry and exchange old troubles for new ones? Hailstones fell everywhere, not only where the avenues of cherry trees stretched over the countryside.

Nowadays, if there is not enough money to enable her to study at a university, a diligent young girl can become a secretary, a receptionist, a physiotherapist, a traveller in refrigerators or baby-wear, a bank clerk, an interpreter, a mannequin, a photographer's model – perhaps in the course of years, actually the manageress of a branch shoe-shop, or the confidential clerk of a bank. But in those days, particularly in a small town, there were no such opportunities. Today there are a hundred and eighty-five different callings for women, I have read in the papers. In those days a girl grew old in service, or else married. Was it not better to sew, wash and cook in one's own home for one's own husband than in a strange household for strange people?

The sisters in the Niedermühle put their heads together and finally decided that one's own troubles are less trying, when all is said and done, than other people's. And so, in spite of all their own worry and trouble, in spite of the work and the crying children, they spent any little free time they had looking out for a husband for their sister Ida.

And as they tried both together and with great determination, they soon found a candidate who seemed suitable. He was twenty-four years of age, worked for a Döbeln saddler, lived in lodgings near by, was industrious and capable, did not drink too much, was saving every halfpenny towards setting up on his own, came from Penig on the Mulde, was looking out for a workshop, a shop and a young wife. And his name was Emil Kästner.

Aunt Lina invited the young man to coffee and home-made cakes on several Sundays at the Niedermühle. In this way he met her sister Ida and he liked her very much. He took her out to dances a few times, but he was not a good dancer so they soon gave that up. He did not mind this. After all, he was not looking for a dancer but for a capable partner in life who would also help him in his future business. And twenty-year-old Ida Augustin seemed just the right girl for him.

For Ida the matter was not quite so simple. 'But I don't love him,' she protested to her elder sisters. Lina and Emma, however, took a dim view of the kind of love one reads about in novels. What did a young girl know about love, anyway? Moreover, love came with marriage. And even if it did not come, it didn't matter all that much; for married life really consisted in working, saving, cooking and bearing children. Love was no more important than a Sunday hat. And one could get through life quite well without a special hat for Sundays.

So Ida Augustin and Emil Kästner were married on July 31st, 1892, in the Protestant church of the village of Börtewitz. And the wedding celebrations took place in the bride's home in Kleinpelsen. The parents and all the brothers and sisters of the bride, and the parents and all the brothers and sisters of the bridegroom, were there. It was a great affair. The bride's father would not let it be said that he was stingy, so there was roast pork and dumplings, and wine, and home-made cakes, and cheese-cakes, and genuine freshly ground coffee. And lots of speeches were made, wishing the young couple happiness, success, plenty of money, and healthy children. The guests touched glasses and drank their health, and were all very sentimental, as is usual on such occasions.

It is curious to reflect on the series of chances which lead up to the fact that one day you lie crying in a cradle and have turned into *you*. If the young saddler from Penig had not gone to Döbeln, but had gone to work in Leipzig or Chemnitz, for instance, and if the young housemaid Ida had not married him but had married a bookkeeper named Pietsch or a plumber named Schanze, I should never have been born. There would never have been one Erich Kästner, who at this moment is sitting in front of his writing-pad trying to tell you about his childhood. Never.

Taking it all in all, I should be very sorry about that. On the other hand, if I did not exist, I could not very well be sorry that I had not been born. But now that I am alive, I must say that I am very glad on the whole. There is a lot of joy in living, though to be sure there is a lot of trouble too. But if you don't live, what do you have? Neither joy nor trouble. Nothing at all. So I'd even prefer to have trouble.

The young couple opened a saddler's shop in the Ritter Strasse, Döbeln. When the door-bell rang Ida Kästner, née Augustin, went into the shop and sold purses, writing-cases, school satchels, briefcases and dog leads. Emil Kästner sat in the workshop and worked. His favourite work was making saddles, bridles, horse-collars, saddle-bags, riding-boots, whips and all leather articles for use with riding-horses, carriage horses and cart-horses.

He was an excellent craftsman, an artist in his craft. And the 'nineties of the last century were extremely favourable years for a young saddler setting up on his own. Wealth was increasing and many wealthy people kept a horse and carriage, or riding-horses. The breweries, factories, building firms, furniture removers, farmers, wholesale merchants and landowners all used horses, and the horses all needed leather equipment. And in the towns round about – in Borna, Grimma, Oschatz – there were cavalry regiments in garrison – hussars, uhlans, horse-drawn artillery, mounted riflemen. All on horseback! And the lieutenants and captains and squadron leaders all had their own horses with particularly smart saddlery. And there were horse-races and gymkhanas and horse-shows all over the place. Nowadays there are lorries, and sports cars, and armoured cars. In those days there were horses, horses, nothing but horses.

My future father was certainly a first-class craftsman, in fact an artist in leather, but he was a bad businessman, and the two were closely related. The school satchel he made for me in 1906 was just as good when I was confirmed in 1913 as on my first day at school. It was then passed on to some other child among our relatives, and continually bequeathed from one to the other as each child left school. I do not know where my good old brown satchel is now, but I should not be surprised if it is still going to school on the back of some small Kästner or Augustin. But that, again, is beside the point. We're still in the year 1892. (And we have to wait another seven years before I come on the scene.)

Anyhow, a man who makes school satchels which never wear out may earn the highest praise, but it's a bad business for him and his trade. If one child wears out three satchels the turnover is considerably higher than if three children use only one satchel. In the one case three children would require nine satchels, in the other case they would need only one. That's quite a difference.

Kästner the saddler made indestructible satchels, briefcases which never ripped, and everlasting saddles for ladies and gentlemen. Naturally his goods were somewhat dearer than elsewhere because he used the best leather, the best thread, and his best craftsmanship. The customers liked his work far better than they liked his prices, and many a one left his shop without having bought.

In fact, the story goes that a captain of hussars wanted to buy a particularly fine saddle in spite of the high price, but my father suddenly refused point-blank to give it up. He liked it too well to part with it, although he could not ride and had no horse. He must have felt like a painter who is asked to sell his best picture but prefers to go hungry rather than deliver it up to strangers. Craftsmen and artists seem to have much in common.

It was my mother who told me the story of my father and the captain of hussars, but when I asked my father about it last summer he said there was not a word of truth in it. Yet I wouldn't mind betting that the story is true.

At any rate the fact remains that he was too good a saddler and too bad a businessman to succeed. The shop did not flourish. The turnover remained low and the overheads remained high. Small debts became bigger debts. My mother took her money out of the savings bank, but that did not help for long.

In the year 1895 the twenty-eight-year-old saddler Emil Kästner sold his shop and workshop at a loss, and the young couple wondered what they should do next. Then a letter came from Dresden from a relative of my father's. Everyone called him Uncle Riedel. He had been a carpenter, had worked for a long time in the building trade, and one fine day had had a bright idea. True, he did not actually invent the block and pulley tackle, but he certainly led the way in applying it to house-building. He was to a certain extent the pioneer in the large-scale application of the block and pulley, and he hired out dozens of block and pulley tackles and other building equipment to smaller building contractors, and made quite a good thing of it.

If you want to know what a block and pulley tackle is you had best ask your father or your teacher to explain it to you. I could do it at a pinch, but it would take a lot of thinking out and a lot of paper. In principle it means that nowadays, instead of every brick and plank being carried up ladders, the stuff is all drawn up by a rope and pulley system worked by a winch, and can be swung in and unloaded at any desired level.

Uncle Riedel earned quite good money with this and later on he gave me many a golden ten- and twenty-mark piece at Christmas and on my birthday. Yes, Uncle Riedel of the block and pulleys was a good man, and so was Aunt Riedel. I mean, of course, Aunt Riedel wasn't a nice man but a nice woman. She had a big china poodle on top of the heating-stove in her living-room. And she also had a rocking-chair.

Uncle Riedel wrote advising his nephew Emil to come to Dresden, the royal residence city of Saxony, since his own business had apparently failed for the time being and he had no very definite plans. But there were other possibilities for a capable saddler. For example, the big decorated travelling bags and hideous chip baskets were completely out of date. The future – and perhaps the future of his capable nephew too – pointed to leather suitcases, and there were already suitcase factories starting up in Dresden.

So my future parents packed up and moved bag and baggage to the Saxon capital, the royal city of Dresden, the city in which I was destined to be born. But I had to wait four more years till then.

4

SUITCASES, CORSETS AND CURLS

DRESDEN was a wonderful city, full of art and history, yet with none of the atmosphere of a museum which happened to house, along with its treasures, six hundred and fifty thousand Dreseners. Past and present lived in perfect unity, or rather duality, and blended and harmonized with the landscape – the Elbe, the bridges, the slopes of the surrounding hills, the woods, the mountains which fringed the horizon – to form a perfect trinity. From Meissen Cathedral to the Castle Park of Groszsedlitz, history, art and nature intermingled in town and valley in an incomparable accord which seemed as though bewitched by its own perfect harmony.

When I was a little boy my father took me for a walk in the Waldschlösschen one fine summer evening because there was a Punch and Judy show there which was my particular delight. Suddenly he stopped and said, 'There used to be an inn here with a very strange name. It was called The Inn of the Silent Music.' I looked at him astonished. The Inn of the Silent Music – that was certainly a strange name. It sounded so odd and so cheerfully crazy that I never forgot it. At the time I thought: Either there's music in an inn or it's silent. But there's no such thing as silent music.

Whenever I stood on the same spot in later years and looked down over the city to the Wielisch and the Babisnauer Poplar, and up the Elbe to the fortress of Königstein, I realized more clearly each time what that innkeeper, who was long since dead and whose inn had vanished into nothingness, had meant. A certain philosopher – I knew that even then – had called the architecture of Dresden, its cathedrals and palaces, 'frozen music'. That Saxon philosopher was really a poet at heart. And an innkeeper, gazing on the silver river and the golden city of Dresden, had christened his inn The Inn of the Silent Music. So it would seem that my Saxon innkeeper had been a poet at heart too.

If it is correct to say that I can not only judge of what is horrible and ugly but also of what is beautiful, I attribute this gift to my good fortune in having grown up in Dresden. I did not have to learn first out of books what is beautiful, neither at school nor at the University. I could breathe in beauty as foresters' children breathe in woodland air. The Catholic Hofkirche, Georg Bähr's Frauenkirche, the Zwinger, Pillnitz Castle, the Japanese Palace, the Jüdenhof and the Dinglingerhaus, the Rampische Strasse with its baroque façades, the Renaissance windows of the Schloss Strasse, the Cosel Palace, the Palace in the Grosser Garten with the Little Houses of the Cavaliers and, looking down from the Loschwitzhöhe, the vista of the city in silhouette, with its noble and venerable towers... But really there is not much sense in reciting the glories that were Dresden like the multiplication table.

I could not describe even a chair so accurately that Kunze the carpenter could reproduce it in his workshop from my description. How then could I hope to describe Schloss Moritzburg with its four round towers reflected in the water, or that sculptured vase by the Italian Corradini near the Palace Pond, almost

Die Frauenkirche

Coselpalais

Hofkirche

Corradini-Vase

Der Zwinger

Zwinger

Schloss Pillnitz

opposite the Café Pollender; or the Kronentor of the Zwinger?
I can see that I shall have to ask the artist to please make a special
set of drawings for this chapter so that you may get at least some
faint idea of how beautiful my native city was.

Perhaps I shall even ask him, if he has time, to draw one of the
little Cavaliers' Houses which flank the Palace in the Grosser
Garten. 'Wouldn't it be lovely to spend your whole life in one
of those little houses?' I used to think when I was a boy. 'Perhaps
you will be famous one day and the Mayor will come with his
golden chain around his neck and present you with one of them
in the name of the city.' And I should have moved into it with all
my books. I should have taken my breakfast in the Palace Café
in the morning, and fed the swans. Then I should have gone for
a walk through the old avenues, down the blossoming rhododen-
dron grove and round the Carola Lake. At midday the cavalier
would have fried himself two eggs and then taken a little nap

by the open window. After that I should have gone to the Zoo, which was only round the corner. Or to the great flower show. Or to the Museum of Hygiene. Or to the horse-races at Rieck. And at night I should have slept soundly, again by the open window, the only living soul in the great old park.

When would I have done any work? you may ask. How can people be so rude and inquisitive? The gnomes, the descendants of the Polish and Saxon court dwarfs, would have seen to that, of course. They are very small but very capable people. With the briefest instructions they would have typed my poems and stories on tiny fairy typewriters while I galloped along the wide, dark brown riding-tracks as far as the Picardie on my favourite steed, the dapple-grey Almansor, and Almansor and I would have had

coffee and cake there. But dwarfs who type poems and horses who eat cake don't belong here!

Yes, Dresden was a wonderful city. You may take my word for it. And you have to take my word for it, because none of you, however rich your father may be, can go there to see if I am right. For the city of Dresden is no more. It has vanished, except for a few fragments. In one single night and with a single movement of its hand the Second World War wiped it off the map. It had taken centuries to create its incomparable beauty. A few hours sufficed to spirit it off the face of the earth. This happened on the night of February 13th, 1945. Eight hundred planes rained down high explosive and incendiary bombs on it. When they had gone, nothing remained but a desert with a few giant ruins which looked like ocean liners heeling over.

Two years later I stood in the midst of that endless desert and could not make out where I was. Among the broken, dust-covered bricks lay the name-plate of a street – 'Prager Strasse', I deciphered with difficulty. Could it be that I was standing in the Prager Strasse, the world-famous Prager Strasse, the most magnificent street of my childhood? The street with the loveliest shop windows? The most wonderful street at Christmas-time? I was standing in a waste half a mile long by half a mile wide, a desert of broken bricks and rubble and utter desolation.

To this day the Governments of the great Powers are disputing with each other as to who murdered Dresden. To this day people are arguing as to whether fifty thousand, a hundred thousand or two hundred thousand lie dead under that desert of nothingness. And none of them will admit having done it: each says it was the fault of the others. Ah, what is the use of quarrelling about it? You will not bring Dresden back to life by so doing – neither its beauty nor its dead. Punish the Governments in future and not the people. And don't punish them afterwards. Punish them at once. Does that sound simpler than it is? No, it is simpler than it sounds.

In the year 1895 my parents moved bag and baggage to Dresden. Emil sKätner, who had wanted so much to remain an independent master-craftsman, became an artisan. The machine age rolled like a tank over handwork and independent craftsmanship. The shoe factories vanquished the shoemakers, the furniture factories the cabinet-makers and joiners, the textile factories the weavers, the china factories the potters, and the suitcase and leatherware factories the saddlers. The machines worked more quickly and cheaply than the craftsmen. Soon there were bread factories and sausage factories and hat factories and jam factories and paper factories and vinegar factories and button factories and pickled-cucumber factories and artificial-flower factories. The craftsmen fought a tenacious rearguard action, and they are still putting up a fight today. It is an admirable struggle, but a hopeless one.

In America the issue has already been decided. Only a few millionaires still go to the gentlemen's tailor who measures his customer thoroughly and requires two or three fittings. All the other men merely go into a shop, take off their old suit and put on a brand new one, lay their money on the counter and go out again. It's as simple as baking biscuits, not like baking biscuits at a baker's, but like baking biscuits in a biscuit factory.

Progress has its advantages, of course. One saves time, and one saves money. But personally I prefer to go to my private tailor. He knows my taste, I know his taste, and Herr Schmitz the cutter knows both our tastes. It is troublesome, expensive and old-fashioned, but we like it that way. And we have many a good laugh during the fittings. I was there again only the day before yesterday. I'm getting a light blue summer suit of a feather-weight material, and it will have a loose-fitting jacket with only a couple of buttons, the second button inside to give the double-breasted effect; width of trousers over shoes nine and a half inches... Oh, good heavens, that reminds me I have to go for a fitting. And here I am sitting at my typewriter. So this time I myself don't belong here!

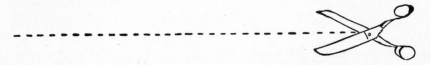

Well, that's done and here I am again. The suit is turning out very nicely, and the three of us are quite satisfied. But where did I leave off? Oh yes, I was still telling you about my future father Emil Kästner and his shattered dream. The old saying 'Handwork is golden', was no longer true. The day of the craftsman's own workshop beside his home was gone for ever. The hungry years of apprenticeship, the lean years as a journeyman, the three anxious years as a master-craftsman on his own had all been in vain. The dream was finished and so was the money. The debts had to be paid. The machines had won.

The alarm clock buzzed at six in the morning. The young man had half an hour's walk over the Albert Bridge, right across Dresden, to Lippold's suitcase factory in Trinitati Strasse. There he worked with other former saddlers, sewing and riveting leather parts together to make suitcases which were all as much alike as peas in a pod. In the evening he came home tired. On Saturdays he brought home his pay-packet. What with new purchases and old debts the money never stretched far enough.

So Ida Kästner, née Augustin, looked around for work – work which she could do at home. For she hated factories as if they were prisons. She thought it bad enough that her husband should have to go into a factory, but that could not be helped. He had had to bow to the yoke of the machine, but she would never, never do so. She would prefer to slave for sixteen hours a day at home rather than work for eight hours a day in a factory. And she did prefer it!

She began making abdominal belts – hard, corset-like linen binders for stout women – for a firm, on piece-work. She lugged home heavy bulky parcels of prefabricated parts and sat bent over her treadle sewing-machine until late into the night, sewing them together. Sometimes the driving-belt jumped off the wheel; the needles broke frequently. It was real sweated labour for a few pence apiece. But a hundred of these belts added up to a few marks, and that helped a little. It was better than nothing.

In the late autumn of 1898 Ida Kästner gave up this home-work and began sewing baby clothes instead. She had always longed for a child, and she had never given up hope that it would be a boy. All her life she had been addicted to being right. And she proved right this time too.

On February 23rd, 1899, at No. 66 Königsbrücker Strasse, towards four o'clock in the morning, after nearly seven years of marriage, she gave birth to a little boy with golden curls. And the matter-of-fact midwife, Frau Schröder, exclaimed, 'My, what a pretty child!'

Ah well, the golden curls did not last for long, but I have still got a faded photograph which shows the future author of certain well-known books sitting on a white bearskin rug dressed in a little shirt. And the infant's head is actually covered with fair silky curls. Since photographs cannot lie the proof seems to be unanswerable. But perhaps you yourselves have noticed how in photographs all people, every single one of them without exception, seem to have ears made too big for them. Much, much bigger than they really are; so big, in fact, that you could imagine them drawing them over themselves at night. So perhaps photographs do play tricks on us sometimes.

Anyhow, whether I was golden-haired or brown-haired, I was baptized shortly afterwards in the beautiful old Protestant Church of the Three Kings in the Haupt Strasse and solemnly given the names of Emil Erich. On Palm Sunday 1913 I was confirmed in the same church by the same Pastor Winter. And a few years after that I became one of the helpers at the children's service there on Sunday mornings. But that doesn't concern us here!

5

THE KÖNIGSBRÜCKER STRASSE AND I

KÖNIGSBRÜCKER Strasse started out pleasantly and inconse-
quently from the complex of thoroughfares – Prager Strasse,
Schloss Strasse, the Augustus-Brücke, Haupt Strasse and the
Albert Platz – which formed the hub of the city. First there was
a pleasant old inn, The Green Fir Tree, with its front garden, and
opposite it a private school for high-class young ladies. At that
time there were still high-class young ladies, as girls whose
fathers had titles or earned a lot of money were called. Perhaps
the girls were so called because they held their noses higher than
others. There were also 'higher schools', and still higher than the
'higher schools' were the high schools or university colleges.

And in other ways, too, people were not particularly unassum-
ing. Superior houses had a notice on their front doors ONLY
GENTLEFOLK ADMITTED, and on their back doors TRADESMEN AND
SERVANTS. The gentlefolk had their own stairs covered with soft
stair-carpets. The servants and tradespeople had to use the back
stairs. If they did not, they were scolded and sent back by the
porter. Little tablets of porcelain on the doors of high-class
apartments declared sternly: NO HAWKERS – NO BEGGARS. Others
were more polite and requested: PLEASE WIPE YOUR FEET.

Almost all these tablets have disappeared since then. They have
died out. So have the bronze or marble goddesses and nymphs

who used to stand about, naked and embarrassed-looking, in halls and on landings, as if they had been ordered and then not called for. Of course, high-class young ladies and upper-class people in general still exist today, but they are not called that any more, and it is not written on door-plates.

In the three houses in which I passed my childhood there were no marble goddesses, bronze nymphs or high-class young ladies. The farther from the Elbe the Königsbrücker Strasse wandered, the shabbier and meaner the houses became. The front gardens became fewer and narrower. The houses became higher, mostly four-storey, and the rents of the flats became cheaper. Then came the 'People's Welfare', a public utility establishment with communal kitchen, communal library and a communal playground which was turned into an ice-rink in winter. After that came the Co-operative Stores, bakers' shops, butchers' shops, greengrocers, little public houses, a bicycle shop, two newsagents, a watchmaker, a shoe-shop and the Görlitz Co-operative Society.

It was in this sector that the three homes of my childhood, Nos. 66, 48 and 38, were situated. I was born in a fourth-floor flat. In No. 48 we lived on the third floor, and in No. 38 on the second. As we went up in the world we moved lower down. We got nearer and nearer to the houses with the front gardens, but we never reached them.

The farther our street went from the town centre, the more its character altered. It traversed the barracks quarter. Just off it, on slightly higher ground, were the Rifle Brigades' barracks, the two Grenadier Guards' barracks, the barracks of the 177th Infantry Regiment, the Horse Guards' barracks, the Army Service Corps barracks, and the two Artillery barracks. And in the Königsbrücker Strasse itself there were the Engineers' barracks, the military bakery, the military prison; and the arsenal, which went up in the air one day.

'The arsenal is on fire!' I can still hear the cry. Flames and smoke hid the sky. The fire engines, the police and the ambulances of the whole city tore along one after another towards the flames and smoke. And behind them, breathless and panting, ran my mother and I. For the war was on and my father was working out there in the military workshops. The flames were eating their way farther and farther, and more and more munition dumps and trains were exploding. Then the area was cordoned off and we were not allowed to go any farther. Anyhow, Father came home in the evening, covered with soot but safe and sound.

Actually, the arsenal fire should not come into this book at all because I was already confirmed then, and no longer a little boy. Yes, and not very long afterwards when I was doing my military service I stood on sentry duty in front of the Engineers' barracks with a rifle on my shoulder. Again in the Königsbrücker Strasse of course. That street and I just could not get away from one another.

We only parted company when I went to Leipzig. Indeed, I should not have been a bit surprised if it had followed me there, we were so inseparable. And whatever else I may have become,

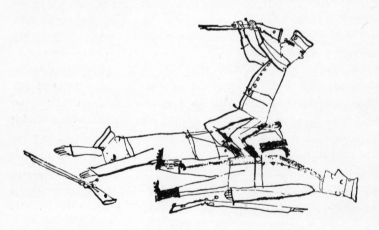

I have always remained a child of the Königsbrücker Strasse, that remarkable street with its genteel houses and front gardens at the beginning, its tenements in the middle, and its barracks, arsenal and the Heller – the sandy drill ground – right at the end of the town. Here on the Heller I played as a boy and did punishment drill as a soldier. Did you ever have to bend your knees two hundred and fifty times holding a rifle Model 98 up in front of you? No? Well, you're lucky! After that a man never really gets his wind back properly for the rest of his natural life. Some of my comrades collapsed after only fifty knee-bendings. They were wiser than I was.

I can no longer remember the fourth-storey flat at No. 66 Königsbrücker Strasse. Every time I passed by the house in later years I thought to myself: 'So that's where you were born.' Sometimes I went into the hall and looked around me with curiosity, but the place rang no bell in my memory. It was an utterly strange house to me. Yet my mother had carried me and the pram hundreds and hundreds of times up and down those four flights of stairs. I knew it. But that made no difference. It remained an absolutely strange building to me, a tenement house like thousands of others.

But I remember No. 48 perfectly well – the vestibule, the window-seat on which I used to sit looking down at the back-yards, the steps of the stairs on which I used to play. For the staircase was my playground. It was here that I used to set up my fort – the medieval fort with the loopholes, pointed turrets and movable drawbridge. Fierce battles took place here. French cuirassiers, after a bold outflanking movement over two steps of the stairs, fell upon the Holksche Rangers and Wallenstein's Musketeers in the rear. Soldiers of the Army Medical Corps, with the red cross on their armbands, stood ready to carry the wounded away on stretchers. They were ready to help all – the Swedes and the Emperor's troops of the seventeenth century just as willingly as the French cavalry of the nineteenth. To my ambulance men every nation and every century were the same. But first the bitter struggle for the medieval drawbridge had to be decided.

There were heavy casualties in these battles. With one movement of the hand I wiped out whole regiments. And Napoleon's Old Guard died to a man rather than surrender. The fighting continued right into the inner courtyards of the fortress after the drawbridge had been stormed. The Nuremburg tin soldiers were tough fellows. And the postman, and little Frau Wilke who lived on the fourth floor, had to take enormous steps, like storks in a bed of lettuce, in order not to endanger either the victory or the defeat. They stepped cautiously over friend and foe, and I took no notice of them at all. For I was Commander-in-Chief and Chief of General Staff of both armies. The fate of all the centuries and all the nations taking part lay in my hands. Was a postman from Dresden-Neustadt going to disturb me? Could he disturb me? Or little Frau Wilke either, just because she had to go out to buy a few turnips and a bit of salt and sugar?

As soon as the battle was decided I used to lay the dead, wounded and unhurt tin soldiers back in their Nuremburg plywood boxes between the layers of wood-wool, dismantle the proud fortress, and carry the toy world and toy history back into our tiny flat.

No. 48 Königsbrücker Strasse, the second home of my childhood! Now, when I shut my eyes here in Munich, I can still feel the steps of those stairs under my feet, and under the seat of my trousers the hard cold edge of the step on which I used to squat, although now, more than fifty years later, they are very different trousers. When I see again in my mind's eye the brown leather shopping-bag, crammed to the brim, which I used to lug up those stairs, I feel the drag first in my left arm and then in my right. For I used to carry the bag in my left hand up to the second floor in order not to hit it against the wall. Then I used to take it in my right hand and grasp the banisters firmly with the left. And finally I breathe a sigh of relief, just as I used to then when I laid the bag down at the door of our flat and rang the bell.

Memory and recollection are mysterious powers, and recollection is the more mysterious and puzzling of the two. For the memory has only to do with our heads. How much is seven times fifteen? And little Paul shouts promptly, 'A hundred and five!' He has learned it and his head has retained it. Or it has forgotten it, in which case little Paul cries, 'A hundred and fifteen!' Whether we know this or that correctly or incorrectly, or whether we have forgotten it and must reckon up anew, good memory and bad memory reside in our heads. The pigeon-holes for all the things we have ever learned are there. I imagine they are like the drawers in a cupboard or a chest of drawers. They often stick when you try to pull them out. Sometimes there's nothing in them, and sometimes there's the wrong thing. And sometimes they won't pull out at all. Then they and we are 'as if nailed down', as the saying goes. Our memories are either large or small chests of drawers. In my own head, for instance, the chest of drawers is rather small. The drawers are only half full, but they're fairly tidy. When I was a little boy my chest of drawers looked quite different. In those days my little top storey was a real lumber room.

Our recollections, on the other hand, do not lie in drawers, nor in cupboards, nor in our heads at all. They live right inside us. They are generally dormant, but they are alive and breathing, and sometimes they open their eyes. They live, breathe and sleep everywhere – in the palms of our hands, in the soles of our feet, in our nostrils, in our hearts, and in the seats of our trousers.

What we have once experienced suddenly comes back after years and years, and stares us in the face. And we feel that it had never gone away at all, it was only asleep. And when one recollection wakes up and rubs the sleep from its eyes, it often arouses others, and they in turn yet others, like sleepers in a dormitory.

There is something very peculiar about one's earliest recollections. How is it that I remember some things from my third year but nothing at all of the fourth and fifth years of my life? How is it, for instance, that I still remember Dr Haenel and the busy nurses, and the little garden of the private clinic? I had cut my leg. The bandaged wound burned like fire; and though I was already able to walk then, my mother carried me in her arms. I cried and she comforted me. And I still remember how heavy I was and how tired her arms became. Pain and fear have a good memory.

 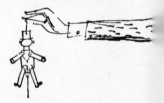

And how is it that I can still remember Herr Patitz and his Studio of Artistic Portrait-Photography in Bautzen Strasse? I was wearing a little sailor frock with a white piqué collar, black stockings which made my legs itch, and laced boots. (Nowadays little girls wear trousers; in those days little boys wore frocks!) I stood at a low table with ornamental legs, and there was a brightly coloured sailing-ship on the table. Herr Patitz stood behind the box camera on its high tripod, stuck his artistic head under a black cloth, and ordered me to smile. When the order remained unheeded he took a jumping-jack out of his pocket and dangled it in the air, crying with desperate jollity: 'Hi! Hi! Look!

Look!' I thought Herr Patitz frightfully silly but I did what he asked all the same, and to please Mamma, who was standing near me, I managed to muster up a shy smile. The photographer now pressed a rubber ball, counted slowly to himself, then shut up the slide and noted the order, 'Twelve copies, postcard size.'

I still have one of those twelve copies with the words: 'My Erich aged three' in faded ink on the back. My mother wrote that in 1902. And when I look at the small boy in the little frock with his round, shyly smiling baby face, neat fringe, and grubby little hand held awkwardly up to his belt, the hollows behind my knees begin to itch again. They are remembering the woollen stockings I was wearing then. Why is that? How is it that they have not forgotten them? Was the visit to the artistic portrait-photographer Albert Patitz really so important? Was it such a sensational event in the life of the three-year-old? I do not think so, but I do not really know. And our recollections themselves? They live and die, and neither we nor they know the reason why.

We often wonder and puzzle about this. We try to raise the curtain a little and get a glimpse at the reasons behind it. All of us, educated or otherwise, try it one time or another, but seldom get beyond puzzling and guessing and conjecturing. My mother and I tried it once too. It was about a boy the same age as myself named Richard Naumann, who lived near us. He was a head taller than I was and quite a nice boy, but he could never stand me. I didn't mind this so much in itself, but I simply couldn't understand why it was, and that was what worried me.

Our mothers used to sit side by side on the green seats in the garden of the Japanese Palace down by the Elbe when we two were in our prams. Later he and I squatted together in the playground making sand-castles. We went together to the Gymnastics Club in Alaun Strasse, and to the higher elementary school. And he never lost a chance of being nasty to me.

He threw stones at me. He tripped me up. He pushed me

backwards until I fell over. He ambushed me from doorways as I passed unsuspectingly, gave me a clout and ran away screeching with joy. I ran after him and whenever I was able to catch him up I made him laugh on the other side of his face. I was not afraid of him, but I couldn't understand him. Why was he always attacking me? Why would he never leave me in peace? I had never done him any harm. I liked him quite well. Why, then, was he always going for me?

One day when I was telling my mother about it, she said, 'Even when the two of you were in your prams he used to scratch your face.' 'But why did he do that?' I asked, baffled. She pondered for a moment, then said: 'Perhaps it was because everyone thought you such a pretty baby. All the old women and park keepers and nursemaids who passed by our seat used to look into your prams, and they always seemed to think you a lot more attractive than he was. They simply raved about you.' 'And you mean to say that he understood that then – when he was a baby?' 'Not the words, of course, but the sense, and the way they said it.' 'And does he still remember that even though he didn't understand it?' 'Perhaps he does,' said my mother, 'and now go and do your home-work.' 'I've finished it long ago,' I answered. 'I'm going out to play.'

And as I ran out of the front door downstairs, I stumbled over Richard Naumann's leg. I raced after him, caught him up and gave him one behind the ear. Perhaps he did hate me since our pram days. Perhaps he remembered them and was not really attacking me, as I thought he was, but only defending himself. All the same I was not going to put up with being tripped by him for that reason – you bet I wasn't!

6

TEACHERS, TEACHERS AND
MORE TEACHERS

I LAY in my cradle and grew. I sat in my pram and grew. I learned to walk, and grew. The pram was sold. The cradle became a laundry basket. My father was still working at Lippold's suitcase factory. And my mother was still sewing abdominal belts. I watched her through the wooden safety railing of my cot.

She sewed until late into the night, and of course the singing noise of the sewing-machine often woke me up. That suited me very well, but it didn't suit my mother at all, for according to parents the proper life's task of small children consists in sleeping as much as possible. And as our doctor, Dr Zimmermann in Radeberger Strasse, was of the same opinion, she gave up sewing the body belts, clapped the polished cover over her Singer sewing-machine, and decided there and then to let a room instead.

The flat was small enough already, but the family purse was still smaller. It would be impossible to carry on without some extra earnings, she told my father, and my father agreed, as he almost always did. They pushed the furniture closer together, cleared out a room, and refitted it for letting. And a cardboard sign, bought in Winter's the stationers, BEAUTIFUL SUNNY ROOM WITH BREAKFAST TO LET AT ONCE. APPLY KÄSTNER, 3RD FLOOR, was hung on the hall door downstairs.

Our first lodger was a primary-school teacher named Franke.

That his name was Franke was of no importance to my future, but the fact that he was a teacher influenced it deeply. To be sure my parents could not know that then. It was just a chance. Our beautiful sunny room might have been rented by a bookkeeper, or a shop-girl, but it attracted a teacher, and it was this chance which was later to prove so significant.

Franke the teacher was a merry young fellow. He liked the room. He liked the breakfast. He liked a laugh, and little Erich amused him. In the evening he sat in the kitchen with us, correcting exercises and telling us about his school. Other young teachers visited him and our home became a lively place. My father stood by the warm stove, grinning contentedly and my mother would say, 'Emil is propping up the stove.' Everyone was as pleased as Punch, and Herr Franke declared that he would never change digs for the rest of his life. And after he had been saying that for a couple of years, off he went and left us.

He married and set up a home of his own. Though this was a very happy reason for giving us notice, we were all terribly sad. He moved to a suburb called Trachenberge, and carried away not only his trunk but also his exuberant laugh. He often came back to visit us with Frau Franke and his laugh. We could hear his laughter as soon as he entered the building, and we could still hear it as we waved after him and his wife from our window.

When he gave notice my mother wanted to hang the sign BEAUTIFUL SUNNY ROOM TO LET on the hall door again, but he said that would be quite unnecessary. He would find someone to succeed him. And he did. His successor was a lady, a teacher of French from Geneva. She laughed much much less than he did, and one day she had a baby. This caused a lot of excitement in our home, and a lot of worry and trouble too. But that doesn't belong here.

★

Mademoiselle T., the French teacher, went away with her little boy soon afterwards, and my mother went off to Trachenberge and told Herr Franke that our beautiful sunny room was vacant again. He laughed and promised her that he would be more careful this time. And so he sent us, for our next lodger, not a lady but a man. A teacher of course, a colleague from his school in Schanze Strasse, a very tall, very fair, very young man named Paul Schurig, who was still living with us when I got my school-leaving certificate. He changed house with us subsequently, and for several years he actually occupied two rooms of our three-roomed flat. So there was not much room left for the three Kästners. But I was allowed to read, write and practise the piano in his room when he was not there.

In the course of time he became a kind of uncle to me, and it was with him that I made my first journey from home. It was in my first school holidays, and we went to his native village of Falkenhain, near Leipzig. His parents had a hardware shop there, and the most glorious orchard I had ever seen. I was allowed to climb up the high ladders and help pick the apples and pears. It was the autumn half-term holiday, and we gathered mushrooms in the woods until our backs ached, and went for lovely walks. And it was up in the attic room in Falkenhain that I wept my first tears of homesickness. There, too, I wrote my first postcard and assured my mother that she needn't be a bit worried about me – there were no trams in Falkenhain, nothing but a dung-cart now and then, and I was very careful of those.

As I have said, the teacher Paul Schurig became a kind of uncle to me as years went by. And he very nearly became a kind of cousin too, because he very nearly married my cousin Dora. She wanted it very much. He wanted it very much. But Dora's father didn't want it at all. For Dora's father was the former rabbit-dealer, Franz Augustin, and he took the dimmest possible view of primary-school teachers and other 'poor starved devils'.

When our lodger, bowing and saying 'My name is Schurig,' presented himself to his hoped-for father-in-law during the presentation of the gold and silver medals at the Grand Horse Show at Rieck, Uncle Franz pushed his brown bowler back off his forehead, coldly eyed the tall, fair, handsome suitor from top to toe, and then, with the memorable words, 'For all I care your name may be Hare!' turned his back on him and us and went off to his prize-winning horses.

This put paid to the lovers' hopes, for there was no opposing my Uncle Franz. And as he suspected my mother of being sympathetic to the project, she got many a rating from him about it. Uncle Franz was a despot, a tyrant, a Napoleon of the horse world. And at bottom he was really a fine fellow. It was not his fault that no one had ever had the courage to stand up to him. He might have been thoroughly pleased if someone had piped up at last and said what he thought. Perhaps he was waiting for this all his life; but no one obliged him. He growled, and everyone trembled. And they kept on trembling, even when he was jovial. They even trembled when he thundered out 'O come all ye faithful' under the Christmas tree.

He enjoyed all this, yet he deplored it. I repeat, in case it hasn't registered, that it was not his fault that no one had ever stood up to him. And with this I shall leave my Uncle Franz and return once more to the real subject of this sixth chapter, namely, school-teachers. We shall meet Uncle Franz again and get to know him better. He would be out of place as a secondary character. He has that in common with other great men, with Bismarck, the founder of the German Empire, for instance.

Once, when Bismarck had convened an international conference and was about to sit down at the conference table with the other statesmen, there was general dismay when it was noticed that the table was a round one. For no matter what you do, it is impossible to seat people according to rank at a round table. But Bismarck smiled, took his seat and remarked, 'The top is always where *I* sit.' Uncle Franz could have said the same. It would not have worried him if there had been only one chair at the table. He would have taken it.

So I grew up with teachers. I did not get to know them only when I went to school. I had them at home. I saw the blue exercise books and the corrections in red ink long before I myself could write and make mistakes. Blue mountains of dictation books, arithmetic books and essay books; and before Michaelmas and Easter, mountains of fawn examination papers. And always and everywhere primers, text-books, teachers' journals, periodicals

dealing with teaching, psychology, folklore and the history of Saxony. When Herr Schurig was not at home I used to slip into his room and sit on the green sofa staring, awestruck yet fascinated, at the expanse of printed and handwritten paper. Here lay a strange continent, so near that I could touch it, but I had not yet discovered it. And when people asked me, as they are apt to ask children, 'What do you want to be when you grow up?' I always answered eagerly, 'A teacher!'

I could not yet read or write, and already I wanted to be a teacher and nothing else. Nevertheless it was all a mistake, indeed the greatest mistake of my life. But I only discovered this when it was almost too late, when, at seventeen, I stood before a class, obliged to teach because the older students of the teachers' training college had gone to the war. The professors, who were looking on as observers, noticed nothing of this. Nor did they notice that I myself had only just realized my error at last, and that my heart was almost standing still. But the children in the benches – they spotted it all right. They looked at me in surprise. They answered well. They put up their hands. They stood up. They sat down. It all went off like clockwork. The professors nodded benevolently. Nevertheless it was all absolutely wrong. And the children knew it. 'That lad up there on the rostrum is no teacher,' they thought, 'and he'll never be a proper teacher.' And they were right.

I was no teacher; I was a learner. I wanted not to teach but to learn. I had wanted to be a teacher so that I could remain a pupil as long as possible. I wanted to absorb new knowledge and to keep on absorbing new knowledge. I certainly did not want old knowledge, nor to spend my life passing on old knowledge. I was hungry, but I was no baker. I was thirsty, but I was no innkeeper. I was impatient and restless, and therefore no future educator of youth. For teachers and educators must be calm and patient. They must think not of themselves but of their pupils. And they must not confuse patience with complacency. There are plenty of teachers who have this kind of patience. But authentic, dedicated teachers are as rare as heroes and saints.

Some years ago I was talking to a Basle University professor, a man famous as a scholar in his subject. He had retired a short time before and I asked him what he was doing now. His eyes shone with sheer delight as he answered: 'I'm studying, now that I have time at last.' At seventy years of age he sat day after day in the lecture halls, learning something new. He was old enough to be the father of the professors to whose lectures he listened, and the grandfather of the students among whom he sat. He was a member of many academies. His name was cited with respect all over the world. He had spent his long life teaching what he knew. Now at last he could learn what he did not know. He was in the seventh heaven of delight. Other people may have laughed at him and thought him a trifle odd, but I understood him as if he were my elder brother.

I understood that old gentleman as my mother had understood me thirty years before when, still in my army uniform, I came to her, feeling utterly dejected and guilty, and said, 'Mother, I cannot be a teacher.' She was a simple woman, and she was a wonderful mother. She was nearly fifty years old then, and she had slaved and pinched and scraped for years so that I could become a teacher. Now the goal was in sight. Only one more examination, which I could easily pass with distinction in a few weeks' time – then she could take her ease at last. Then she could fold her hands in her lap, because I would be able to earn my living. And now I came to her and said, 'I cannot be a teacher.'

It was in our big living-room, one of the two rooms which the teacher Schurig occupied. Paul Schurig was sitting in silence on the sofa. My father was leaning in silence against the stove. My mother was standing under the lamp with the green silk shade and the pearl fringe. And she asked, 'What would you like to do, then?' 'Get my matriculation at a high school and then go on to the university to study,' I said. My mother pondered for a moment. Then she smiled and nodded. 'Very well, my boy,' she said. 'You shall study!'

*

But there, I have been thrusting my hand into the wheel of time again, between the spokes of the future. Again I have run ahead of the calendar. Perhaps I should write: 'But that doesn't come in here at all!' I should be wrong, however. For a great deal of what one goes through as a child only reveals its meaning many years later. And a great deal of what happens to us in later life would be practically incomprehensible to us except in the light of our childhood memories. Our years and decades interlock like the fingers of clasped hands. Everything links up with everything else.

The effort to tell the story of one's childhood turns into one of those processional dances where one has to take three steps forward and two steps back; and the readers, poor creatures, have to dance too. I cannot help that. And little side jumps like this one are unavoidable too. Now we take two steps back again, to the time when I was not yet going to school and nevertheless had already decided to be a teacher.

In those days if a boy was clever and his father was not a doctor, solicitor, pastor, officer, businessman, or manager of a factory, but only an artisan, a workman or a clerk in an office, his parents did not send him to a grammar school and then on to the university. That would have cost too much. Instead they sent him to a teachers' training college. He went to the elementary school until he was confirmed, and then sat for his entrance examination. If he failed he became a bookkeeper or clerk like his father. If he passed he entered the college and was an assistant teacher six years later. He received a salary, could begin to help his parents, and had a 'pensionable position for life'.

Aunt Martha, my mother's younger sister and my favourite aunt, was also in favour of this plan. She had married a certain Herr Richter, a widower with two daughters, who was foreman of a cigar factory. She also had a child of her own, an allotment garden, six hens and a very merry heart. She always had a lot of trouble, yet she was always cheerful. Two of the three daughters, her own golden-haired Helene and one of the step-daughters, died of typhus caused by undernourishment in the first year after the First World War. Even though we had so many butchers in the family. But there I am going two steps ahead again!

Aunt Martha also said, 'Make a teacher of Erich. Teachers have a grand time. You know that yourselves. Look at your lodgers, Franke and Schurig, and Schurig's friends the Tischendorfs.' The Tischendorfs were Paul Schurig's friends, and they were teachers like himself. They often came to visit him and sat in the kitchen with us. Or the three of them would pore over maps in the front room, planning their summer holidays. For four weeks of the year they became mighty mountaineers. Every summer they went off to the Alps with climbing boots and ice-picks, crampons, ropes, first-aid kits and enormous rucksacks, and they climbed Mont Cenis in France, Monte Rosa in Switzerland, the Marmolata in the Dolomites, the Kaisergebirge in Bavaria, and the rest. They sent glorious brightly coloured picture postcards back to the Königsbrücker Strasse. And when they came back at the end of the holidays they looked like blond Negroes — tanned a dark brown, full of beans and ravenous as wolves. The floor-boards sagged under their nailed boots. The table sagged under the plates of sausages and fruit and cheese they consumed. And the rafters sagged when they told of their experiences in scaling mountain ridges, peaks and precipitous faces, and their crossing of crevasses in glaciers.

'And they have Christmas holidays and Easter holidays and half-term holidays as well,' said Aunt Martha. 'They give a few hours' lessons in between, of course, but they're always the same lessons and always for the same age-group. They correct thirty exercise books or so, go to the Zoo with their class and tell the children that giraffes have long necks, draw their salary on the

first of the month, and sit back peacefully, waiting to retire.'
Teaching is not quite such an easy and pleasant profession as all
that, but my Aunt Martha was not the only one who thought it
was. Many others did too; and so did many teachers. Not every
teacher was a Pestalozzi.

So I wanted to be a teacher, and it was not only because of my
hunger for education. I had a fine healthy appetite for other things
too. And when I helped my mother to get Herr Schurig's supper,
and carried his plate of three fried eggs, sausages and ham into the
front room, I thought to myself: 'A teacher doesn't do half
badly!'

And the fair-haired giant Schurig had no idea how joyfully
I would have exchanged my supper for his.

7

GYMNASTICS AND SWEETMEATS

MY book and I are making headway. I have already been born, which is the main thing. I have been photographed. I have moved with my parents into a new home, and I have been surrounded by teachers ever since. I don't yet go to school. I have teachers at home — but not tutors. They do not teach me my tables, not even 'once one is one'. But I carry sizzling fried eggs on warmed plates into our best room, which is no longer our best room, but theirs. 'When I am big', I think, 'I will be a teacher. Then I can read all the books I like and eat as many fried eggs as I like!'

A year before I went to school I became, at barely six years old, the youngest member of the Neustadt and Antonstadt Gymnastics Society. I had given my mother no peace until she had allowed me to join it. She was dead against it. She said I was too little. But I plagued her, harried her, tortured her and pursued her with my pleading. 'You must wait until you're seven,' she had always answered.

And one day I found myself standing before Herr Zacharias in the smaller of the two gymnasiums. The rows of boys were just doing general exercises. 'How old is the boy?' he asked. 'Six.' 'You must wait until you're seven,' he said, bending down to me.

76

My answer was to clench my fists in front of my chest, spring to the feet astride position, and start a solo display. He laughed, and the lines of boys laughed too. The whole hall resounded with laughter, and Herr Zacharias said to my astonished mother, 'All right, buy him a pair of gym shoes. The first lesson will be at three on Wednesday.' I was overjoyed. We went straight into the nearest shoe-shop and that evening I wanted to go to bed with my gym shoes on. When Wednesday came I was in the hall an hour before the time. And what do you think Herr Zacharias was by profession? A teacher, of course. A teacher in a teachers' training college. I was his pupil there later and he laughed many a time over our first meeting.

I was an enthusiastic gymnast and I became a pretty good one. I was soon an expert with dumb-bells, the Indian clubs, the climbing-rack, the rings, the parallel bars, the horizontal bars, the vaulting-horse, the box, and finally, the high horizontal bars. Later, indeed much later, the high horizontal bars became my favourite gymnastic exercise. I enjoyed the swinging, circling, supporting, straddle-sitting, circling while hanging from the knees on the horizontal bar, and finally the flight through the air, and the landing on the coconut matting and scrambling to one's feet. It is a glorious sensation to feel one's body, attached only by the firmly gripping hands, becoming lighter and lighter in a rhythmic swing until it seems to have no weight at all as it flashes round a firm yet pliant bar in fantastic curves.

I became a pretty good gymnast. I shone at displays and was leader of the team. But I did not become a very good gymnast because I was terrified of swinging right over the high horizontal bar, and I knew why. I had been present once when another boy had lost his hold in full swing and fallen down head first. The comrades who were standing around had been unable to catch him in time, and he was carried off to hospital. And for the rest of my life I sedulously avoided swinging right over the high horizontal bar. That was really a very disgraceful thing, and who likes being disgraced? But I never got that fear out of my system and preferred to bear disgrace rather than risk a fractured skull. Was I right? I was.

I wanted to do gymnastics because I enjoyed them. I did not want to be a hero. And I did not become one — either false or real. Do you know the difference? False heroes have no fear because they have no imagination. They are stupid, and they have no nerves. Real heroes have fear, but they overcome it. Many and many a time in my life I have been afraid, and God knows I have not overcome my fear every time. If I had done so I might perhaps be a real hero today, but I should certainly be a dead one. Now I do not want to make myself out worse than I really am. I have been quite brave at times, and it was not always easy. But being a hero would never have done as my main calling.

I did gymnastics because my arms, legs, hands and body wanted to play and develop themselves. My body wanted to be trained like my mind. Both demanded simultaneously and imperiously to be trained to grow limber and supple, keeping pace in growth and strength like healthy twins. I was sorry for all the children who loved study but did not love physical exercise. I pitied all the children who loved gymnastics but did not love study. There were even some children who did not want either to do gymnastics or to study and I was sorriest of all for these. I was absolutely desperate to do both, and I was already looking forward to the day when I would go to school. But when the day came, I wept.

The Higher Elementary School in Tieck Strasse, not far from the Elbe, was a tall gloomy building with one entrance for girls and another for boys. In those days all schools looked gloomy, stern and dismal, and were dark red or blackish-grey in colour. They had probably been built by the same contractors who built the barracks. They looked like barracks for children. Why the builders did not think of making more cheerful-looking schools I do not know. Perhaps the façades, staircases and corridors were meant to inspire us with respect like the teacher's cane and the rostrum. The idea in those days was to train children, by means of fear, to be submissive citizens; by fear and terror, and that was certainly all wrong.

The school did not frighten me. I did not know any cheerful-looking schools. Doubtless they had to be as they were. And Herr Bremser, the stout pleasant teacher who welcomed the mothers and fathers and the new pupils did not frighten me at all. I knew from home that even teachers could laugh, eat fried eggs, look forward to their long holidays and have their little afternoon nap. So there was nothing to make me tremble.

Herr Bremser put us in rows according to size, and took down

our names. The parents stood close-packed along the walls and in the gangways, nodding and smiling encouragingly to their sons and holding the paper cones of sweets. This in fact was their chief task. They held small, medium or giant cones in their hands, compared the size of each other's cones and were proud or envious accordingly. You should have seen mine! It was as gaily coloured as a hundred picture postcards, as heavy as a coal bucket, and reached right up to the tip of my nose. I sat contentedly in my place, beaming at my mother and feeling a prince of cone-owners. Some of the little boys were crying in the most heart-rending fashion and running to their excited mammas.

But it was all over soon. Herr Bremser bade us goodbye and parents, children and paper cones set out noisily for home. I carried my cone of sweets like a flag-standard before me. Now and then I laid it down on the pavement and rested. From time to time my mother seized it and carried it for a bit. We sweated like furniture removers. Even a sweet load is still a load.

In this way we helped each other along through Glacis Strasse, Bautzener Strasse, across the Albert Platz and into Königsbrücker Strasse. From Luisen Strasse onwards I refused to let the cone out of my hands any more. It was a triumphal procession. Passers-by and neighbours stared. Children stopped and ran after us, swarming round us like bees that smell honey. 'And now let's go to Fräulein Haubold!' I said to my mother from behind my cone.

Fräulein Haubold was the manageress of a branch of a well-known dyer's in the ground floor of our tenement house, and I spent many hours in the quiet, spotless room. It smelled of freshly ironed clothes, chemically cleaned gloves and starched blouses. Fräulein Haubold was an elderly spinster, and we liked one another very much. I had heard that she said nice things about me, so she deserved the glorious sight better than anyone else. That went without saying.

My mother opened the door. With the paper cone and its red bow of ribbon pressed against my face I mounted the step into the shop, but as I could see nothing through the cone and its bow, I stumbled, and the tip of the cone broke off. I stood as still as a pillar of salt – a pillar of salt clutching a funnel of sweets whose contents poured in a steady rustling stream over my laced boots. I raised the cone as high as I could. This was not difficult because it was getting lighter and lighter. Finally I found myself holding nothing but a brightly coloured bottomless cardboard funnel. I lowered it and looked down at the ground. I was standing ankle deep in sweetmeats – chocolate creams, dates, Easter hares, figs, oranges, tartlets, waffles and golden cockchafers. The children who were following us giggled. My mother covered her face with her hands. Fräulein Haubold gripped the counter. What an abundance of sweetness! And I was standing in the middle of it.

You can shed tears over chocolates and sweets, especially when they happen to be yours. We hurriedly stuffed the sticky wreckage of sweets and fruit into my beautiful new brown leather school satchel and tottered through the shop, out of the back door to the well of the stairs, and up to our flat. Tears obscured the childish heaven. The contents of the paper cone were glued together in one sticky mass in the satchel. Two presents had melted into one. My mother had bought the beautiful paper cone and filled it with good things. My father had made the satchel. When he came home in the evening he cleaned it. Then he took his sharp saddler's knife and cut out a little bag for me. It was a little bag with an adjustable strap and was made of the same indestructible leather as the satchel. I carried my mid-morning snack to school in it ever afterwards.

The journey to school was a more formidable matter than the school itself, for there was only one grown-up person in the class-room — namely, Herr Bremser himself. No doubt he was there because he had to be. Without him we could not have learned the letters and figures, the A B C and the once-times table. But to have Mother take me by the hand and deposit me at the school door was most annoying. At seven one was not a baby any more. Who would dare to say he was? Frau Kästner dared; she was a brave woman. But she dared it only for eight days, for she was a clever mother. She gave in; and I marched off every morning to Tieck Strasse armed with satchel and tuck bag, proud and alone and every inch a man, and home again at midday. I had won. Hurrah!

Many years later my mother told me what really happened. She waited until I was out of the house. Then she quickly put on her hat and coat and ran secretly after me. She was dreadfully afraid that something might happen to me on the way, yet she would not thwart my growing desire for independence. So she hit on the idea of seeing me to school without my knowing it. When she feared I might turn round she darted quickly into a doorway or behind a hoarding. Or she hid behind stout people who were walking in the same direction, and peered round them, never letting me out of her eye. The Albert Platz with its trams and drays was her biggest worry. But she was not completely easy about me until, watching round the corner of Kurfürsten Strasse, she saw me disappear into the school. Then she breathed a sigh of relief, set her hat straight, and walked home sedately instead of stalking like a Red Indian on the warpath. But after one week she gave up her morning manœuvres, for she now felt convinced that I would not be careless.

One little difficulty remained, however — to get me out of bed in good time. That was no easy task, particularly in the winter, when it was still dark outside. She thought up a musical reveille. She sang 'Erich — get up — go to school!' and she kept on singing it until I gave way, with much grumbling and eye-rubbing. When I shut my eyes now I can still hear that sing-song, first pleasant, then becoming more and more threatening. But the little song did not really cure me. Even now I find it hard to get out of bed.

I just wonder what I would think if, walking into town early one morning, I saw a pretty young woman suddenly darting behind a hoarding before my eyes; if I followed her out of curiosity and noticed her stalking behind stout people, now quickly, now slowly; darting into doorways, peering round corners. And if I noticed that she was following a little boy who was crossing streets and squares carefully all alone, after looking correctly to left and right. Would I think: 'Has the poor creature gone crazy?' or 'Am I watching a tragedy?' or 'Is a film being shot here?'

No, I should know what it was all about. But do such things happen nowadays? I have no idea for, as I say, I am not an early riser.

In school itself there was only one difficulty. I was dreadfully inattentive. School was too slow for me. I was bored stiff. So I carried on entertaining conversations with my neighbours in front, behind and beside me. Clearly young men of seven have a lot to tell each other. Herr Bremser, easy-natured though he was, found my love of chattering most disturbing. His efforts to make thirty little Dresdeners into good readers were sadly hampered by the fact that one-third of the class was carrying on unlawful conversations, and that I was the ringleader. Finally he lost patience one day and told me angrily that if I did not mend my ways he would write to my parents about me.

When I came home at midday I imparted this interesting information. 'If I don't mend my ways', I repeated, still out on the landing taking off my satchel, 'he will write a letter to you. His patience is at an end.' My mother was really horrified at this account of things, and still more by the coolness with which I repeated it. She took me very seriously to task, and I promised her that I would behave better. I could not guarantee that I would become attentive there and then and for ever, but I would not disturb the other pupils in future. That was a fair offer.

And the next day my mother went to Herr Bremser unknown to me. When she had told him everything he laughed. 'You don't say so!' he cried. 'What an odd boy. Any other child would have simply waited and said nothing until his parents got the letter.' 'My Erich keeps nothing back from me,' my mother answered proudly. Herr Bremser nodded and said, 'Well, well.' Then he asked: 'Does he know what he wants to be when he's grown-up?' 'Oh yes, a teacher,' she replied. At this he nodded again and said, 'Yes, he's clever enough.'

At the time I heard nothing of this interview with my teacher, but I kept my word and did not disturb the classes any more. I even went further and tried to be as attentive as possible, though I had given no promise to do so. And by the way, I act in exactly the same way today. I prefer to promise too little rather than too much. And I prefer to do more than I have promised rather than less. As my mother used to say, 'Everyone is odd in a different way.'

When a child has learned to read and likes reading, he discovers and conquers a new world, the world of letters. The land of reading is a mysterious, endless continent. Things, people, spirits and gods we could never see otherwise come to life for us by printer's ink. The child who cannot yet read is only aware of what is under his nose – his parents, the door-bell, the lamp-lighter, the bicycle, a bunch of flowers; and from the window, perhaps the church tower. The child who can read sits over a book and suddenly he can see Mount Kilimanjaro, or Charles the Great, or Huckleberry Finn on the prairie, or Zeus transformed into a white bull with the fair Europa riding on his back. The child who can read has a second pair of eyes, as long as he takes care that he does not spoil the first pair.

I read and read and read. Nothing printed was safe from my eyes. I read books and pamphlets, advertisements, titles of firms, name-plates, catalogues, directions for use, inscriptions on tombstones, animal lovers' calendars, menu cards, Mamma's cookery book, greetings on picture postcards, Paul Schurig's teachers' journals, the *Coloured Picture-Book of Saxony* and the wet scraps of newspaper in which I carried home heads of lettuce.

I read as I breathed — as if I would suffocate if I didn't. It became an almost dangerous passion with me. I read what I could understand and what I could not understand. 'That is not for you,' my mother would say; 'you will not understand it.' But I read it all the same. And I thought to myself, 'Do grown-ups understand all they read?' Now I am grown-up myself and I can answer with authority as an expert: grown-ups do not understand everything they read either. If they only read what they understood the printers and compositors in the newspaper offices would be permanently on short time.

8

A DAY IN THE LIFE OF AN
EIGHT-YEAR-OLD

FIFTY years ago, as now, the day was only twenty-four hours long, and I had to sleep during ten of those hours. The rest of the time was filled up like the engagement book of a managing director. I ran to school in the Tieck Strasse. I went to Alaun Strasse and did gymnastics. I sat in the kitchen and did my home-work, at the same time keeping an eye on the potatoes to see that they did not overcook. I took my midday meal with my mother and my evening meal with both my parents, and I had to learn to hold my fork in the left hand and my knife in the right. That was none too easy because I was and still am left-handed. I tucked in quickly and then had to wait ages until my turn came for another helping, because I was a little boy and must not push myself forward. I went into town with Mamma and had to stand in front of a whole lot of shop windows which did not interest me in the least. I played with Fritz Forster or Erna Grosshenning in some backyard. I also played cops and robbers, or palefaces and Indians with Gustav Kiessling on the edge of the Heller, among the pine-trees, sand and heather. On Bischofs Platz I supported the Königsbrücker gang against the dreaded Hecht gang, a horde of warrior urchins from Hecht Strasse. And I read, and read, and read.

Grown-up people don't get through half as much. When I'm writing a book I don't find any time to read books. If I try to read, I go short of sleep, and if I have enough sleep I am late for my appointment at the Four Seasons Hotel. Then my whole day's schedule goes awry. My secretary has to wait half an hour for me before I arrive at my habitual café to dictate some urgent letters. And when I have done that, or at least half of it, I arrive late at the cinema, or I don't go at all. I never seem to come to terms with time. It has become too narrow and too short, like a quilt which has shrunk in the wash.

Children get through a lot more; and all the time they keep on growing. Many of them shoot up like asparagus. I certainly did not do that. My achievements in learning, reading, gymnastics, doing the shopping and peeling potatoes far excelled my abilities in growing. When I last stood to be measured the sergeant-major of the Army Medical Corps said to the corporal who was noting my measurements on my army passport, 'Five feet five and a half inches!' That is a miserable height for a man. But Caesar, Napoleon and Goethe were also small, and the great painter and artist Adolf Menzel was even smaller. When he was sitting down he looked as though he were standing up. And when he stood up from a chair, people thought he was sitting down. It is cheering to think how many small men are numbered among the great.

I loved school, and in the whole course of my school life I never missed a single day. It was almost a record-breaking passion with me. I marched off in the morning with my satchel on my back whether I was well or as hoarse as a crow, whether my tonsils or teeth pained me, whether I had stomach-ache or a boil on my seat. I wanted to learn and never to miss a day. I postponed more serious illnesses to the holidays. On one occasion only I almost gave in. That was due to an accident, and it happened this way.

One Saturday I had been to my gymnastics class and on my

way home I had bought a bunch of flowers for Sunday from little
Frau Stamnitz, and as I entered the hall I heard someone scrub-
bing the stairs a few floors up. Knowing from my mother's household routine that it was she, I ran up three steps at a time, shouting
'Mamma!' loudly and joyfully, slipped, and fell right on my chin,
still shouting and therefore with my mouth open. The steps were
made of granite; my tongue was not.

It was a frightful business. I had bitten right through the edges
of my tongue. Dr Zimmermann, the kind family doctor with the
turned-up moustaches, could tell us no more at first because my
tongue was so swollen that it filled up my mouth like a dumpling
– an infernally painful and by no means tasty dumpling. The
wounds would have to be stitched, Dr Zimmermann said, because
the tongue is an indispensable muscle for speaking, eating and
drinking. My tongue to be stitched! My parents and I almost
fainted with horror, and Dr Zimmermann did not seem very
happy about it either. He had known me since I was born, and he
would have preferred to stitch his own tongue together with a
needle and thread rather than mine. First he ordered me to rest in
bed and have camomile tea. It was not a very pleasant night. There
was hardly room in my mouth for even ten drops of camomile
tea; I found it impossible to swallow, and sleep was quite out of
the question. It was just the same on Sunday too.

But on the Monday morning, weak and shaky though I was, I
tottered off to school against the wishes of my parents and the
doctor. No one could have held me back. My mother walked
along with me, worried and exhausted, told the teacher what had
happened, begged him to keep an eye on me, and then, with a
last look at my bloated face, left the utterly flabbergasted teacher
and class.

It took six weeks to heal. For three weeks I lived on milk, which
I sucked with difficulty through a glass tube. For three more weeks
I lived on bread and milk. During the mid-morning break I sat

alone in the classroom, my face distorted with pain in my efforts to swallow, and listened to the noise and laughter from the school playground. During lessons I remained dumb. Sometimes, when no one else knew the answer, I wrote it on a bit of paper and carried it up to the teacher's desk.

My tongue did not have to be stitched after all. The swelling went down gradually and after about six weeks I could eat and speak again. Two scars remained, one at each side, and I still have them today. In the course of the years they have become smaller and gone nearer to the roots of my tongue. But don't ask me to show them to you; I don't put out my tongue at my readers.

The Heller, where we played in the summer, was not far away, and yet it led from the labyrinth of streets into a completely different world. We picked bilberries amid sweet-smelling heather. The pine trees waved silently over our heads. The soft summer breeze wafted over the smell of freshly baked Army bread from the Army bakeries. Sometimes the slow train to Klotzsche lumbered down the line or a couple of armed soldiers escorted a squad of sulky-looking prisoners back to the military prison from their stint of penal labour. They wore drill suits, had no cockades on their caps, and the sand crunched under their wooden shoes.

We watched them as they walked over the level-crossing and disappeared into the prison. Many of the cell windows were barred, others were nailed up with dark brown boards so that only a little bit of daylight could find its way into the cells. We heard that the ones convicted of serious crimes were behind those nailed-up windows. They could not see the sun, nor the pine trees, nor us children tired of playing Red Indians in the flowering heather, but they could hear, as we did, the whistles of the trains as they passed the signal box. What crimes had they committed? We did not know.

The little bells of the heather smelled sweetly, and so did the Army bread. The trains whistled. The signalman, having finished watering his flowers, set his peaked cap straight and awaited the passing of the next train with correct official deportment. The train snorted by. We waved at it until it disappeared around the bend. Then we went home – to our tenement flats. Our parents, Königsbrücker Strasse and our supper awaited us.

Otherwise we played in the backyards, performed gymnastic feats round the carpet poles and had our afternoon snacks thrown down to us from the kitchen windows. It was like something in a fairy-tale to watch them hurtling through the air wrapped in paper and plopping on the pavement. They were only sandwiches spread with liver sausage or pork dripping, but to us they seemed like manna falling from heaven. Ah, how wonderful they tasted! Never in my life have I eaten anything better, not even in the Baur au Lac in Zürich or the Ritz Hotel in London. But it wouldn't help a bit if I asked the head waiter to have the pâté de foie gras truffé spread on rolls and flung out of the window to me on to the hotel terrace. For even if he consented to do it for a really big tip, it would still be nothing like those rolls spread with pork dripping.

When it was wet we used to play in the vestibule of the house or in the loft over Kiessling's stable, where it smelled delightfully of chopped straw, hay and clover. Or we climbed into the delivery cart, cracked our whips, and drove wildly, rattling and rumbling over the prairies. Or we chatted to the stamping horse in the stable. And we often visited Gustav's father, the butcher, in the slaughter-house where he worked with his apprentices among wooden troughs, pigs' intestines and cauldrons of sausages. We liked it best on Fridays because the black puddings and liver sausages were cooked, stirred and filled that day, and we were allowed to sample the mixture as expert tasters. Our judgment was impeccable, particularly on the Kiessling speciality, hot garlic sausage.

Even now, as I sit at my typewriter, my mouth waters at the memory of it. But it's no good. Hot garlic sausage is no longer made, even in Saxony. Perhaps the butchers of my childhood days had the recipe buried with them in their Sunday frock-coats? If so, it was a grave loss to the civilized world.

For a time I was passionately addicted to playing billiards. The father of a school friend of mine had an inn near the Johann-stadt Embankment. It was deserted in the afternoon while the father had his nap upstairs in his flat and only the barmaid remained on duty in case any thirsty wanderer should stray in. She washed glasses behind the counter, made us sugar beer or ordinary beer with raspberry juice in it, gave each of us a long wooden spoon to stir it, and then we retired sedately to the inn parlour. Here there was a billiard table.

We hung our jackets over the backs of chairs because the coat-stand was too high for us. Then we picked the smallest billiard cues we could find among the selection standing by the wall, and

stood on our toes to do the marking because the cues were too long and thick and also much too heavy. It was an arduous business. The billiard table was too high and too wide for us. The ivory balls never got properly rolling. To get a right screw into the ball we had to lie half over the edge of the table with our legs dangling. To write our scores on the slate we had to get up on a chair. We tortured ourselves like Gulliver in the land of the giants, when really we should have been laughing at ourselves. We didn't laugh at all, however, but went about our game with solemn dignity, like grown-up men competing at the tournament for the Central German billiards championship. We found this solemnity great fun.

But it all came to an end one fine day when we made a hole in the green baize. I cannot remember which of us was the unlucky culprit, he or I. I only know that suddenly there was a big triangular tear in the precious cloth. I slunk away utterly crushed. That evening my school friend received the expected hiding from the practised paternal hand, and there was an end for ever to our billiard tournaments and sugar beer. I have forgotten the name of the inn and the street, and even the name of my school friend. It has fallen through the big holes of the great sieve. Where to? Into the emptiness which remains empty, no matter how much falls into it. Memory is unjust.

Children delight in play-acting. Little girls change their dolls' nappies and scold the infants. Little boys stick aluminium saucepans on their heads, put on deep voices, and all of a sudden they are valiant knights or mighty emperors. And grown-up people, too, love disguising themselves and making themselves grotesque, especially at carnival time, when they buy, borrow or make costumes, and go dancing dressed as Eastern slave girls, men from Mars, Negroes, apaches or gipsy girls, and behave quite differently from their real, everyday selves.

This happy talent has never been mine. I cannot get out of my skin, as the saying is. I can invent characters, but I have no wish to portray them. I love the theatre with all my heart, but only as a spectator. And when I stick on a moustache and go to the carnival as Kaiser Wilhelm, I do so because I don't want to be a spoilsport; and I just stand or sit about the hall like a painted idol, not joining in the fun and games at all but only looking on. Is it that I'm too shy or too solemn? I don't really know.

But there has to be an audience too. If no one sat in the stalls the actors would not have to don their wigs and crowns at all. They would have to take their make-up boxes to the pawnshop and look for an occupation that does not require an audience. So it is really lucky that there are some of my kind.

My career as a spectator began very early and that was due to a chance. I was seven or eight years old when my mother met a certain Frau Gans at Frau Wähner's, the milliner's, and became friendly with her. Frau Gans was an impressive lady. Despite her name – Goose – she was more like a swan or a peacock than a goose. She was the lady friend of an actor and had two little daughters. The elder one, who was gentle and beautiful as a flower, was nearly always ill in bed, and faded away, gently and beautifully, while still a little girl. The other daughter, Hilda, was neither beautiful nor gentle, and had a temperament like a gala firework. This wild temperament of hers burst from every seam and bore her along, indomitably and inevitably, towards one single goal – the stage.

Little Hilda Gans acted all the time, whether she was walking or standing, and whether she had an audience or not. And when we went to visit them in the Kurfürsten Strasse her public consisted of four persons – her mother and mine, her invalid sister and myself. She began her performance by playing the box-office girl and selling us tickets. She squatted in the open doorway between the bedroom and the living-room, with a scarf over her head, and handed us scribbled bits of paper in exchange for a suitable payment. The front row cost two pfennigs, the second row one.

The difference in price was really not necessary at all, because her sister was in bed in any case, and the rest of the audience would have had to take up very awkward positions if they had wanted to spoil one another's view. But the correct procedure had to be observed and Hilda, now turned usherette, firmly showed those who only paid one pfennig into the second row of chairs. In her role of usherette, by the way, she wore no head-scarf, but only a white bow.

As soon as we were seated the performance began. The troupe of players consisted solely of the artiste Hilda Gans, but that did not matter. She played every type of role – old people, children, heroes, witches, fairies, murderers and virtuous maidens. She disguised and transformed herself on the open stage. She sang, jumped, danced, laughed, shouted and wept with such energy that the living-room shook. The prices of the seats were certainly not too high. We got a marvellous variety entertainment for our precious money. And we heard again and again from the bedroom the wheezy, thin laugh of the gentle little invalid sister.

The gentleman friend of Frau Gans, the mother of the young artiste, had formerly been a distinguished actor himself and now had a job in the management of the two theatres run by the Dresden municipality. One of them was the open-air theatre, which was in the middle of a wood, surrounded by a high close board fence. Performances were held here on three afternoons of the week. The audience sat round in a semicircle on primitive wooden benches enjoying fairy-tales, popular plays, comedies and farces. There was a smell of pine needles. Ants crept up one's stockings. Spectators outside stuck their noses over the fence. The summer purred like a cat in the sun.

Sometimes thick black clouds rolled up and we looked anxiously at the sky. The thunder growled and the players raised their voices against the unfair competition which became ever louder and louder. And sometimes the clouds burst, the lightning shot out like tongues of fire, and the rain gushed down on the last act. Then we fled, and the players, too, sought cover for themselves and their costumes. Nature had vanquished art.

We stood with our coats over our heads under the great trees which swayed in the storm. I pressed close to my mother and while I became wetter and wetter tried to guess the end of the play of which the elements had so maliciously cheated us.

The other theatre run by the municipality was in the Trabanten Gasse, and was independent of the heavens. We were regular patrons of this one also. Here, too, there were real plays. And here little Hilda Gans trod the boards for the first time. She played the title role in a stage version of Hauffs' marvellous fairy-tale, *Dwarf Nose*. She played it with a hump on her back, a red wig, an enormous false nose, a squeaky treble voice and a temperament which simply knocked the audience over. Even Mother and I, experienced Hilda Gans experts though we were, were completely carried away – not to mention Mother Goose, I mean Mother Gans.

This success sealed the fate of my friend Hilda Gans. While still a child she went on the stage, took singing lessons and became a soubrette. As the name Gans did not sound very suitable for a singer, she called herself Inge van der Straaten from that time onwards. Why she has not become famous I do not know. Life has its mysteries.

Soon the theatres of Dresden became my home from home, and Father often had to eat his supper alone because Mamma and I were paying homage to the muse Thalia, generally in standing places. We took our supper during the long interval, standing in the corners of the stairs. There we unwrapped our sausage sandwiches, and the sandwich papers, neatly folded, disappeared into Mother's brown handbag again.

We frequented the Albert Theatre, the Playhouse and the Opera. We queued for hours in the street to grab the cheapest places when the box-office opened. When we failed we went home as shattered as if we had lost a battle. But we did not lose many battles. We won our standing places by guile and patience and held out bravely in them. Anyone who has ever literally stood through Goethe's *Faust* or one of Wagner's operas will surely take off his hat to us. Only once did my mother faint, and that was at *The Mastersingers* one hot summer afternoon. By this mishap we actually got two seats – they were on the step of the last row – and we were able at least to hear the dance of the apprentices in the last act.

My love of the theatre was love at first sight, and it will remain my love until my last breath. I have written many theatrical critiques, and now and then a sketch or a play. Opinions may differ about these efforts, but there is one thing about which I will permit no contradiction – as a spectator I cannot be beaten.

9

THE LITTLE MULTIPLICATION
TABLE OF LIFE

THE first years at school passed by peacefully and pleasantly. Herr Bremser did not have to be too cross with us, and we children were well satisfied with him too. The school reports were distributed with ceremony before the Easter holidays. The parents were invited to be present, and we sang children's songs and recited poems from our school readers for their entertainment. I wore a velvet suit on special occasions in those days, and I seemed to be always in demand for recitations. So when I stood up and went into the middle of the hall, the grown-ups used to nod and smile at each other and whisper: 'Little Velvet Suit is in it again this time!' I was Little Velvet Suit of course. And Frau Kästner would sit bolt upright, bursting with pride. Unlike me, she had no stage fright and not the least fear that I should falter or fail. She was right, as always. I did not forget my lines. My school reports, too, were always excellent. On the way home we used to go into a restaurant where I was treated to cream cakes and crackle cakes and hot chocolate. (Do you know what crackle cakes are? No? Oh, you poor creatures!)

As I wanted to be a teacher and was going to be one, ways and means had to be planned quite early on. And they were planned betimes. My education was going to cost a lot. The years in the training college would cost money. The college fees would cost money. The piano lessons would cost money. And the piano itself would also cost money. I still remember quite clearly that it cost exactly eight hundred marks second-hand. That was a fortune!

Long before this my father had begun repairing handbags and briefcases for neighbours and relatives at the week-ends at home; also soling shoes, stitching ripped school satchels and suitcases, and making indestructible purses and notecases which delighted his customers. He used to sit by the kitchen window on his cobbler's stool, with a cigar in his mouth, working tirelessly with  tacks, sandpaper, tags, waxed thread, cobbler's wax and needles, hammer, knife, shoemaker's last, bending-tool and folding-stick. And the gluepot stood on the stove beside the pot of noodle soup. Do you know what boiling glue smells like – and in the kitchen of all places? It may smell like rose-water to a saddler, but to a woman standing at the stove in the evening cooking the next day's dinner it stinks like a thousand unwashed devils. The noodle soup, the beef, the haricot beans and the lentils – everything she cooked, according to Mother, reeked and tasted of glue. And there must be an end to it!

So my father was banished from the kitchen paradise and went into exile. From now on he spent his evenings down in the cellar, behind the lath and plaster partition, among the coals, briquettes and potatoes, wearing a woollen cardigan and thick felt slippers. The cellar was his workshop now. Here the smoke from his cigar rose in rings. Here the bubbling glue boiled on a spirit-stove. And both the glue and my father felt much better.

It was down here too that, at seventy years of age, he made a

life-sized horse with the aid of many a pot of glue. A horse with glass eyes but with a real mane and tail. And its saddle, bridle and reins were gazed at with awe and wonder by the inhabitants of the whole tenement. Seated on this horse, which could be guided by hand because the noble beast had rubber-tyred wheels in place of hooves — seated on this racehorse my father planned to take part in the carnival procession. Unfortunately his plan came to nothing because the motive power, a septuagenarian pal of his who was to propel horse and rider from underneath the saddle cloth, went down with flu just at the crucial moment. And so the beautiful plan fell through. But my father bore this disappointment too with his characteristic patience. His patience failed very, very seldom in his patient life. He was always a master-craftsman and almost always a master in the art of smiling too, to the very end.

My father did not build any life-sized horses while I was a little boy. He was too busy trying to earn as much money as possible so that I could become a teacher. And he worked and earned as much as he was able, but that was too little.

So my mother decided to learn a trade. And when my mother decided on anything, no one dared to get in her way. No chance and no fate would be so presumptuous. Ida Kästner, who was already thirty-five, decided to take up a trade, and she took it up. Neither she nor fate batted an eyelid. The greatness of a human being does not depend on the size of his or her field of action.

This is a fundamental truth from the little multiplication table of life, but it is seldom mentioned in the schools.

In spite of her age my mother decided to become a hair-dressing apprentice with a view to setting up as a hairdresser on her own when trained. Not with a shop, because that would have cost too much, but with a licence to carry on the trade of hair-dresser – waving, shampooing and scalp massaging – in her own home. The official of the hairdressing trade whom she approached made all sorts of objections. She would not admit any objection, so no objection existed. Finally she was referred to one Herr Schubert, a well-known ladies' hairdresser in the Strehlener Strasse. Here, with talent and the utmost application, she learned all that was to be learned, and for many weeks she only came home, tired but happy, in the evening after the shop was closed.

During this time I was alone a great deal. At midday I had my dinner for fifty pfennigs in the People's Municipal Restaurant. There was self-service here, and since you had to provide your own knife and fork, I brought mine with me in my school satchel. At home, armed with Mamma's bunch of keys, I played

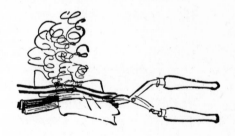

housewife, did my homework, brought home the shopping, carried up wood and coal from the cellar, pushed briquettes into the heating-stove, made coffee, and drank it with Paul Schurig when he came home. And while he was having his afternoon nap on the green sofa, I went out to the yard to play. When he had gone out again I washed and peeled the potatoes, sometimes cutting my finger in the process, and then read until dark.

Or sometimes I walked right through the town and called for my mother at Schubert's. When I arrived too early through fear of being late, I sat watching her wielding the curling-tongs, first trying it on a piece of tissue paper and then on the customer's mass of hair. For at that time women still wore long hair. Many of them had hair that reached to their knees. It smelled of perfume and birch-water. The customers gazed unwaveringly into the mirror, critically observing the coiffure which was coming into being under Mamma's skilful hands with the aid of pads, postiches, brilliantine and hairpins. Sometimes the master-hairdresser, Herr Schubert, in his white coat, would come and stand beside his pupil and her handiwork, and compliment her or give a momentary hand himself. And from week to week he expressed himself more and more satisfied with her.

Finally he informed the Hairdressers' Guild that his pupil had learned all that was required from him, that she possessed a great deal of skill and taste for the work, and that, as master-hairdresser and holder of gold and silver medals, he advocated the candidate's admission to the Guild. Accordingly Frau Ida Amalia Kästner, née Augustin, received a document in which 'the aforementioned' was authorized to call herself an independent hairdresser and to trade as such. That evening I was sent out to the restaurant Sibyllenort at the corner of Jordan Strasse for two litres of beer, and the victory was celebrated in style.

As there was no other space available, the front left-hand corner of the bedroom was fixed up as the hairdressing salon, and equipped with a wall mirror, a lamp, a wash-basin, an electric point for the drier, and gas brackets for the heating of the curling-tongs. A hot-water supply had to be bravely forgone. It would have cost too much. I was entrusted with the task of producing

hot water for the shampooing on the kitchen stove. And in the years that followed I certainly carried thousands of jugs of water from the kitchen to the bedroom.

Combs and brushes, friction towels and hand towels, liquid soap, shampoos, brilliantine, hairpins, curlers, hairnets, postiches, massage oils and creams had to be purchased. Business cards had to be distributed. A porcelain business plate was screwed on to the hall door downstairs. Appointment cards for waves and massages were printed. There were all sorts of things to be thought of.

Finally, Aunt Martha had to lend her head for a few days. The elder sister dressed, massaged and waved the younger one until both were quite exhausted with effort and laughter. The fingers of the hairdresser and the head of the 'customer' were both sore. But this final rehearsal was necessary. There can be no première without a dress rehearsal. Only after this may the public come. And the public came.

Frau Wirth the baker's wife; and Frau Ziesche, another baker's wife; Frau Kiessling, the butcher's wife, and Frau Kletsch, who had a greengrocer's shop; and the wives of the plumber, bicycle dealer, carpenter, florist, druggist and stationer; the wife of the tailor Grosshennig, the draper's wife, and the ironmonger's wife; the wives of the restaurant owner, photographer, chemist, wine merchant, coal merchant, laundryman, dairyman; as well as the daughters of all these ladies, the manageresses of the chain stores and the shop-girls – they all streamed in. First, because they had to look trim behind their counters, second, because there were not many ladies' hairdressers in our neighbourhood; third, because we were their customers, and fourth, because my mother was a competent hairdresser and gave them good value for their money.

She had all she could do to cope with them. Business flourished, and often I had to watch and see that the midday meal did not burn up completely. 'Take your dinner, Erich,' she would call from the next room. But I would wait on, turn the gas down to a glimmer, spoon water into the steaming saucepans, get the frying-pan ready, lay the table in the kitchen, and then go on reading until finally the door closed on the last customer, after a lengthy conversation out on the landing.

My mother also carried on her trade outside the home. When she had to do this she packed her implements and the spirit-stove into her attaché case and dashed off, sometimes to the other end of the town. These professional excursions were undertaken mainly for regular 'appointment customers'. These had to be treated with particular consideration as they were, of course, the backbone of the business. Some of them actually paid for ten or twenty waves or massages at a time! These appointment customers included the wife of a rich jeweller, but also a poor little huckster. And actually I remember the latter particularly well.

Her name was Fräulein Jaenichen, she lived in Turnerweg, in a miserable room over a public house, and she could not dress her own hair because she was a cripple. Her hands, and her feet too, were twisted and crooked. In fact, her whole body was bent and crippled. No one bothered about the poor wretch so she had to fend for herself. She hobbled about the countryside on one short and one long crutch with a heavy basket on her hunched back, selling all sorts of small goods – buttons, garters, safety-pins, trimmings, buckles, aprons, whetstones, gas lighters, sewing-silk, knitting-wool, crochet mats, penknives, pencils and so on.

And just because she looked so dreadful, the poor creature was especially keen on having her hair nicely waved.

Mother had to be out of the house before six in the morning. Very often I went with her because this seemed to help her to endure the stuffy room and the sight of the pathetic creature. Half an hour later we helped Fräulein Jaenichen to shoulder the heavy basket with its broad leather strap. Then she crawled at a snail's pace to Neustadt Station, propped on the two unequal crutches, and travelled out to the villages on a suburban train. Bent over and swaying from side to side, she staggered along by the railway line in the cold early morning air and took ten times longer to get there than other people. In fact, she moved so slowly that she looked as though she were stamping and treading on the same spot.

Weddings, too, brought big business. They meant visiting the bride's home and dressing the hair of ten, twelve and sometimes even fifteen females – the bridesmaids, the mother, the mother-in-law, the sisters, aunts, friends, grandmothers

and sisters-in-law; and of course the all-important bride herself. The homes were poky and packed with excited people. Wine was handed round. The cheese-cakes were burning in the oven. The dressmaker was late in delivering the bridal dress. The bride was in tears. The bridegroom came too early. The bride's tears flowed faster. The bride's father was in a bad temper because he couldn't find his best collar studs. The women, dressed in taffetas and silks, chattered incessantly. It was 'Frau Kästner' here and 'Frau Kästner' there, and meanwhile the hairdresser was as likely as not pinning on the bride's veil and hurriedly cutting half a yard off because it was too long.

Now the bridal carriage drew up before the door and the groom and his best man ran down with bottles of beer to make the drivers more patient. But even this could not help matters much, because the parson at the church could not wait; he had more marriages to follow this one. But where on earth were the bouquets, and the baskets for the little flower girls? And where were the girls themselves? In the kitchen, of course, getting themselves well smeared with cocoa! Where was the stain remover? Where was the top-hat case? Where were the little camellia blossoms for the buttonholes? Where were the hymn-books?

At last the door of the flat was slammed. At last the carriages rolled off to the church. At last the flat was empty – or almost. The neighbour who had promised to mind the roast in the oven now began to draw the tables together, collect the chairs, and lay the wedding-table with the beautiful damask cloths, the Dresden china, the silver and the gleaming cut-glass wineglasses, and the flowers artistically strewn over the cloth.

Meanwhile my mother sat at the kitchen table, with tired feet and aching hands, drinking coffee, sampling the cakes, stuffing a bit into her big handbag for me and counting her earnings and tips. She had pains in every limb. Her head was in a whirl. But this wedding job had been worth while. She had the next instalment for the piano in hand; and the fee for the next few piano lessons for Fräulein Kurzhals.

Fräulein Kurzhals lived in the same house as we did, but two flights higher, and she was very dissatisfied with my progress, alas with reason. For the costly decorative piece of musical furniture was in Paul Schurig's sitting-room. When he was in his school, I was in mine. When I was at home, he was generally at home too. When was I supposed to practise? Yet I simply had to learn to play the piano since I was to be a school-teacher.

One feeble ray of comfort remained to me. Paul Schurig played the piano abominably, and in spite of that he had become a teacher. So there!

10

TWO FATEFUL WEDDINGS

THE strangest wedding I ever remember became graven in my memory because it did not take place at all. And that was not because the bridegroom had said 'No' before the altar or fled from the church. It was because there wasn't any bridegroom at all. The best thing will be to tell the story right from the beginning.

One day an oldish spinster named Fräulein Strempel came and told us that she was going to be married the following Saturday in St Paul's Church. And she made an appointment with my mother for eight o'clock on that morning. No. 27 Oppel Strasse, two flights up, the left-hand flat. Ten heads of hair were to be done. The bridal carriage and five cabs had been ordered. The Hotel Bellevue was undertaking the catering, with iced soufflé for desert and a waiter in a dinner jacket. Fräulein Strempel's eyes shone with joy as she chattered on eagerly like a young girl. We congratulated her on her good fortune, and when she was gone we congratulated ourselves on ours. But we did so too soon.

When I came home from school on the Saturday my mother was sitting in the kitchen utterly cast down and red-eyed. She had reached No. 27 Oppel Strasse at eight o'clock sharp, rung the bell on the left-hand door two storeys up, but been greeted with astonished stares, and angrily sent away. No Fräulein Strempel lived there and there was no one being married at twelve o'clock in St Paul's Church!

Had my mother taken down the house number incorrectly? She inquired in the shops round about. She asked in the neighbouring houses. She rang at all the doors. She turned the whole of Oppel Strasse upside down. No one knew Fräulein Strempel, and there was no one waiting to have her hair done or going to be married at midday. Some of the people she asked were very nice and polite to her, but not one of them was as obliging as all that! So now we sat in the kitchen and just wondered. We realized that we had been duped, but why – why on earth had this woman humbugged us? She had injured my mother. But what good had it done her?

A few weeks later I saw her again. I was coming out of school with Gustav Kiessling; and she passed us by without recognizing me. She seemed to be in a hurry, so there was no time to lose. It was now or never. I quickly slipped my satchel off my back, gave it to my friend and whispered, 'Here, take this home and tell Mother I'll be home later.' And off I ran after the woman. Gustav stared after me, then went on, and dutifully brought home my satchel. 'Erich is coming later,' he reported. 'Why's that?' asked my mother. 'No idea!' answered Gustav.

Meanwhile I was playing detective. Since Fräulein Strempel (whose name was probably not Strempel at all), had not recognized me, the matter was simple enough. I did not have to hide nor put on a beard, so why whould I be in such a hurry to tackle her? I had only to keep on her heels. Even that was not quite simple, however. For Fräulein Strempel (or not-Strempel) was in a great hurry and had long legs. We made good headway.

Albert Platz, Haupt Strasse, Neustadt Markt, Augustus Brücke, Schloss Platz, the Georgentor, Schloss Strasse – the journey seemed endless. But quite suddenly it came to an end. The lady turned left into the Altmarkt and disappeared behind the glass swing doors of Schlesinger & Co., a high-class ladies' fashion shop. I plucked up courage and followed her. How it was all going to end, I did not know, and I felt painfully embarrassed when the manager, the lady supervisors and the salesladies all fixed their eyes on me. But what was I to do? She walked across the ground floor, the ladies' coats department. So did I. She went up the stairs, passed the first storey, the costumes department, and climbed the next flight. So did I. She entered the department on the second floor, summer frocks and junior miss department, went up to a wall mirror, pushed it aside — and disappeared! The mirror swung back to its old spot behind her. It was like something out of *The Arabian Nights*.

I was now standing in the midst of counters, mirrors, movable wardrobes and leisurely salesladies, and felt rooted to the spot by my fright and my sense of duty. If only there had been some lady customers there trying on or buying things. But it was midday,

and the ladies were at home, not at Schlesingers. The shop
assistants began giggling. One of them came up to me and asked
playfully, 'What about a smart little frock for the young gentleman? We have some charming models in stock. Wouldn't you
like to come into a cubicle and try some on?' The other girls
laughed and held their hands to their mouths. Silly creatures!
How was it that Fräulein Strempel (or not-Strempel) had disappeared behind this mirror? And where was she now? I felt as
though I were standing on hot coals. A minute can be very long.

But here was another of these vile females coming up to me.
She took a brightly coloured gown from a stand, held it under
my chin, squinting as if examining it, and said, 'The cut shows off
her wonderful figure to the best advantage!' The other girls
nearly split their sides laughing. I got red in the face and furious,
but at that moment an elderly lady appeared on the scene and a
dead silence fell on the whole department. 'What are you doing
here?' she asked me sternly. As I could think of nothing else to
say, I answered, 'I'm looking for my mother.' 'Not one of us,
duck!' one of the girls cried, and the laughter broke out again.
Even the elderly lady almost smiled.

At this moment the wall mirror moved noiselessly aside and
Fräulein not-Strempel walked out of it, without her hat and coat.
She smoothed down her hair, said to the others, 'It seems to be
lunch-time still in here,' and went behind one of the counters.
So she was a saleslady at Schlesingers, on the second floor. But I
was already on the stairs; I had decided to go straight down again
and find the manager. This called for a man-to-man discussion!

Having listened to my story the manager told me to wait a
few minutes. Then he went up to the second floor and returned,
after five minutes, with Fräulein not-Strempel. She had her hat
and coat on again, and she looked through me as though I were
made of glass. 'Now listen to me,' said the manager. 'Fräulein

Nitzsche will go back home with you and come to an arrangement with your mother to compensate her in instalment payments. Here's a card with Fräulein Nitzsche's address. Put it away
safely and give it to your mother. Tell her she may call to see me
any time if it's necessary. Goodbye.'

The glass doors swung open and shut again. Fräulein Nitzsche
alias Strempel and I were out in the Altmarkt. Without deigning
to look at me she turned into Schloss Strasse and I followed her.
It was a frightful march. I had won and yet I was utterly wretched
about it. I felt like one of those armed soldiers who walked behind
the military prisoners on the Heller. I was proud and ashamed at
the same time. That can happen. Schloss Strasse, Schloss Platz,
Augustus Brücke, Neustadt Markt, Haupt Strasse, Albert Platz,
Königsbrücker Strasse – on she went, straight as an arrow, in
front of me. I followed, keeping five paces behind all the time,
even up the stairs. At the door of our flat she turned towards the
wall. I rang three times. My mother came rushing to the door,
wrenched it open, and cried, 'Now I want to know at last why
you ... !' Then she noticed that I was not alone and saw whom I
had brought. 'Please come in, Fräulein Strempel,' she said.
'Fräulein Nitzsche,' I corrected her.

They came to an arrangement for three monthly instalments,
and Fräulein Nitzsche, still completely impassive, went back to
Schlesinger & Co. with a confirmation from my mother in her
handbag. The loss was made good – nevertheless it was a
catastrophe, as we found out in the course of time. Creditors
turned up on all sides. The hotel, the wine merchants, the cab
owner with the wedding carriages, the flower shop, the laundry –
all alleged that they had incurred loss and all demanded that part
of the loss be made good by instalment payments. And Fräulein
Nitzsche went on paying it off, for months and months.

Luckily she kept her job at Schlesingers, for she was a capable saleslady and the manager had understood what I could not understand as yet. An ageing spinster who had not found a husband and would have liked to marry had invented a wedding when her wish had not come true. It was a costly dream and a fruitless one; and when she woke up from it she started paying for it in instalments. And with every month's instalments she grew a year older. We often met in the street but we did not look at one another. We had both done right and wrong, but I had come out of it the better. For she was paying for a dream which was at an end, but I was still a little boy.

Another wedding which I remember brought us much more trouble, although it was not an ill-starred dream, but duly took place. This time the bridegroom was no invention. He existed, and he made no attempt to run away. But the bride's home and the church were in Niederpoyritz, far down the valley of the Elbe. And it was a hard, ice-cold, pitiless day sometime between Christmas and the New Year.

I waited for Mother in the local inn. I sat and ate and read, and the hours crawled by. They slouched wearily round the glowing iron heating-stove. The world outside the windows was greyish-white and barren, and the wind was sweeping the fields like a drunken porter, driving the cold, crusted snow from one corner to another. It sent it whirling about like dust in the air, and it howled and bawled, making the window-panes clatter. Again and again, as I looked out, I thought to myself, 'It must be like that in Siberia.' Yet it was only Niederpoyritz, near Dresden on the Elbe.

When my mother came to fetch me after five hours, she was so exhausted by her work that she felt she could not trust herself to sit down and rest. She insisted on starting for home at once, so we set out on our way. It was a way without a way; a day without light. We sank into the snow-drifts. The storm buffeted and ambushed us from all sides and made us stagger. We held one another fast. We froze to the marrow of our bones. Our hands went dead. Our feet felt as if made of wood. Our noses and ears became white as chalk.

Just as we neared the tram stop the tram moved off in spite of our shouting and waving. The next one did not come for twenty minutes. It was unheated, and covered with snow. During the whole journey we sat silent and stiff, side by side, our teeth chattering. When we got home my mother went to bed and stayed there for two months. She had terrible pains in her knee joints. Dr Zimmermann said it was synovitis and ordered compresses of boiling hot water.

During those weeks I was her nurse and I scalded my hands again and again and dressed the scalds with mashed potato. I was cook, and when I came home from school at midday I concocted dinners of scrambled eggs, rissoles, roast potatoes, rice and noodle soups with beef, or kidneys and herbs, lentils with saveloys, even roast beef with mustard and raisin sauce. I was waiter, and I served my over-salted, badly cooked and burned masterpieces with pride but without skill on Mother's bed. In the evening I laid a cold meal ready for Paul Schurig and many a time I secretly cut off a slice of sausage for myself. For our own supper I fetched the meals in big pots from the municipal restaurant, and when my father came home from the suitcase factory we warmed up the food. After the meal we washed up and Paul Schurig helped with the drying. We clattered the plates and cups so noisily that we gave Mother, listening from the bedroom, many a start.

Sometimes we even did the washing and hung it up on a line we had strung across the kitchen. Then, crouching like Red Indians on the warpath, we crawled under and between the dripping handkerchiefs, shirts, sheets, towels and underpants, and felt them every quarter of an hour to see whether they were dry

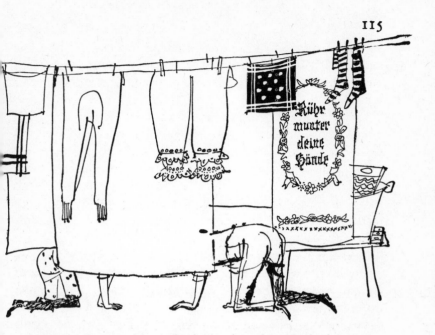

at last. But they could not be hurried, and we had to wipe up many a pool with the floorcloth lest the lino should get marked.

It was a real bachelor household and my mother suffered not only from the pains in her knees but also on our account. She was afraid for the crockery. She was afraid I would starve. And she was afraid her customers would be unfaithful to her and turn to her rivals. This third anxiety was not unjustified, for a ladies' hairdresser had set up in Eschen Strasse and was canvassing all the shops round about for their staffs' custom. So Mother had to hurry up.

Dr Zimmermann declared that the patient was still ill. The patient asserted that she was well, and it was a foregone conclusion which of the two would prove right. She got up, clenched her teeth, surreptitiously held on to the furniture when she walked about, and was well. I trotted round from shop to shop announcing the glad tidings. The rival hairdresser was defeated. The household recovered its equilibrium. Life resumed its old course.

11

A CHILD'S TROUBLES

THERE are many clever people in the world and they are often right. Whether they are right when they assert that children should definitely have brothers and sisters because otherwise they grow up too much alone, are spoiled, and remain self-centred eccentrics all their lives, I do not know. But even clever people should refrain from making sweeping statements. Twice two is always and everywhere four – in Djakarta, on the island of Rügen, at the North Pole. And that was so even in the far-off days of the Emperor Barbarossa. But things are different in the case of many other axioms. People are not arithmetical examples. What is true of little Fritz may not be true of little Karl.

I remained the only child of my parents and I was entirely satisfied with this arrangement. I was not pampered and I did not feel lonely. Of course I had friends. Could I have loved a brother any more than I loved Gustav Kiessling, or a sister more deeply than my cousin Dora? You can choose friends for yourself, but you cannot choose brothers and sisters. You choose friends freely, on your own, and when you both perceive that you have made a mistake, you can part. Such a severance hurts, for there is no anaesthetic for it. But the operation is possible and it is also possible for the wound in the heart to heal.

With brothers and sisters it is different. You cannot choose them for yourself. They are delivered to the house. They arrive cash on delivery and cannot be sent back. Destiny does not send brothers and sisters on approval. Luckily brothers and sisters can become friends. Frequently they remain only brothers and sisters. Sometimes they become enemies. Life and literature have many beautiful and moving but also many sad and terrible stories to tell on this subject. I have heard and read many of them; but I cannot contribute any myself. For I remained, as I have said, the only child, and I was satisfied with this.

Only once in every year did I ardently wish to have brothers and sisters – on Christmas Eve. For all I would have cared they could have packed up and flown away again on Christmas Day after the roast goose and dumplings, the red cabbage and the celery salad. I would gladly have given up my own helping of goose and eaten giblets instead if only I did not have to be alone on the evening of the twenty-fourth of December. They could have had half my presents. And what truly glorious presents they were!

Why did I not wish to be alone and not to be an only child on this, the most beautiful evening of a child's year? Because I was afraid. I dreaded the presentation of the gifts. I dreaded it, and I dared not show that I did. It is not surprising if you do not understand this right away. I have been pondering for a long time past whether I should speak of it or not. But since I am going to speak of it, I had better explain it to you.

Their love of me made my parents jealous of each other. They tried to hide it, and they often succeeded. But on the most beautiful day of the year they did not succeed. At all other times they were so careful to get on well together for my sake, but on Christmas Eve they simply could not manage it. It was beyond

their power. I knew all about it, but for the sake of all three of us I had to behave as if I did not know it.

For weeks beforehand my father had sat down in the cellar half the night making, for instance, a wonderful toy stable for me. He had carved and nailed, glued and painted, done miniature writing, cut and sewn miniature harness, plaited through the horses' manes with ribbons, filled the mangers with hay and, down there by the smoky paraffin lamp, had thought again and again of something else to add – another joint, another band or clasp, another hook, another broom for the stable, another box for the oats, until at last, grinning contentedly, he was able to say to himself, 'It takes me to do a job like that!'

Another time he made a dray complete with beer barrels, a drop ladder, wheels with hub-covers and iron rims – a solid vehicle with wheel axles, and interchangeable shafts according to whether I wished to yoke one horse to it or two; with leather cushions for letting the beer barrels down on and whips and brakes at the driver's seat. And this toy, too, was a faultless masterpiece, a work of art.

These were gifts at the sight of which even little princes would have clapped their hands with joy. But my father would not have given them to princes.

For weeks on end my mother spent half the day roaming through the town searching the shops. Every year she bought so many gifts that her hiding-place, the chest of drawers, bulged.

She bought roller-skates, building-bricks, coloured pencils, tubes of paints, painting-books, dumb-bells and clubs for the gym class, a football for playing in the yard, ice-skates, musical tops, hiking-boots, a Norwegian sledge, a little box of precision instruments on blue velvet, a little printing-press with a set of compositor's letters and, under the guidance of Paul Schurig and the Teachers' Guild of Saxony, a great many good children's books. And of course quantities of handkerchiefs, stockings, gym shorts, knitted caps, woollen gloves, sweaters, sailor blouses, swimsuits, shirts and similar useful things.

It was a rivalry in their love for me and it was a bitter one. It was a drama with three characters, and the last act took place every year on Christmas Eve. A little boy played the principal part. Whether the piece turned out a tragedy or a comedy depended on his talent in improvisation. Even now when I think of it, my heart is in my mouth.

I sat in the kitchen and waited to be called into the best room, under the Christmas tree, for the presentation. I had my own presents ready — a little box of ten or perhaps twenty-five cigars for Papa; for Mamma a scarf, a watercolour drawing painted by myself or — as happened once when I possessed only sixty-five pfennigs — the 'seven articles' beautifully packed in a cardboard box from Kuhne's drapery. What are 'the seven articles'? A reel of white and a reel of black sewing-silk, a packet of pins and a packet of needles, a spool of white thread, a spool of black thread, and a dozen medium-sized black press-studs — seven different articles for sixty-five pfennigs! That, I thought, was a record achievement. And I would have been proud of it if I had not been so afraid at the time.

I stood at the kitchen window and looked at the windows opposite. Here and there they were already lighting the Christmas candles. The snow on the street shone in the light of the street-lamps. I could hear Christmas carols. The fire was crackling in the heating-stove, yet I was freezing cold. The kitchen smelt of raisin buns, vanilla sugar and candied peel, yet I felt utterly miserable. But at any moment now I should have to smile, though I felt much more like crying.

And then I heard my mother call, 'Now you can come!' I grabbed the prettily wrapped presents for the two of them and went into the passage. The door of the best room stood open. The Christmas tree was lit up. Father and Mother had taken up their positions to right and left of the table, each beside their own gifts as if the room and the festival had been divided in half. 'Oh, how beautiful!' I exclaimed, meaning both halves. I still kept near the door so that my efforts to smile happily would be taken as referring unmistakably to both. Papa, with the cigar gone out in his mouth, beamed at the brightly varnished stable. Mamma looked triumphantly down at the mountain of gifts on her right. We all three smiled in an effort to smile down our triple uneasiness. But I could not go on standing at the door.

I walked hesitantly up to the glorious but, alas, divided table, and with every step my feeling of responsibility, my fear and my determination to get over the next quarter of an hour successfully grew stronger. Ah, if I could only be alone, alone with the presents and with the heavenly feeling of being doubly loaded with gifts — gifts from a united love! How lucky I should have been, and what a happy child! But I had to play my role so that the Christmas drama should end happily. I was a diplomat, more grown-up than my parents, and it was up to me to see that our solemn Three-Power Conference under the Christmas tree should pass off without discord. Already at five or six, and still more so later on, I was the master of ceremonies of Christmas Eve, and I performed the heavy task with considerable aptitude, but with a trembling heart.

I stood at the table and expressed my joy in a shuttle movement. I showed joy towards the right, to the delight of my mother. Then I showed joy towards the left of the table, over the toy stable, in a general way. Then I showed joy to the right again, this time over the toboggan; and then to the left once more, taking particular notice of the leather harness. And once more to the right, and once more to the left, never too lengthily, never too hurriedly. I rejoiced sincerely, but I had to divide up and dissemble my joy. Then I gave each of them a kiss on the cheek. My mother first. I presented my gifts, beginning with the cigars. In this way, while Papa was opening the box with his penknife and sniffing the cigars, I was able to stand a little longer beside my mother than beside him. She admired my gift and I gave her a little secret hug, as secret as if it were a sin. Had he noticed it? Was it making him sad?

Next door in the Grüttners' flat they were singing 'O Come, All Ye Faithful'. My father took out of his pocket a purse he had made down in the cellar and held it out to my mother, saying, 'I had almost forgotten this.' She pointed to her half of the table, on which were socks, long woollen underpants and a tie for him. Sometimes we were already eating our sausage and potato salad before they realized that they had forgotten to give each other their gifts. And Mother would say, 'It's time enough after supper.'

Afterwards we went over to Uncle Franz's, where we had coffee and raisin buns. Dora showed me her presents. Aunt Lina complained a little about her varicose veins. Uncle picked up a box of Havana cigars, held them under my father's nose and said, 'Here, Emil. Smoke a decent cigar for a change!' And Papa answered, slightly offended, 'I have some myself, thank you.' Then Uncle Franz said a trifle crossly, 'Go on – take one! You don't get 'em like that every day.' And my father said, 'Very well, if I may.'

The housekeeper Frieda, a faithful soul, brought buns, ginger cakes and Rhenish wine, or steaming punch if the day were extra cold, and sat down with us at the table. Dora and I tried to play Christmas carols on the piano, and the 'Petersburg Sleigh Ride' and the 'Skaters' Waltz'. And Uncle Franz began to talk about the rabbit-trading days to annoy Mother. He mimicked the sister telling tales on her brothers. My mother defended herself as best she could, but there was no defence possible against Uncle Franz. 'You were a tell-tale-tit!' he roared, and cried boisterously to my father, 'Your wife was too grand for us by half, even as a child, Emil!' My father smiled quietly over his spectacles, took a sip of wine and wiped his moustache, wholeheartedly enjoying the fact that my mother, for once, did not have the last word. That was the best Christmas present he could have. Her cheeks were flushed from the wine. 'You were low, deceitful, lazy rascals!' she cried furiously. Uncle Franz was delighted that he had succeeded so well in annoying her. 'Well, maybe we were, Duchess,' he replied,

'but we have made good all the same.' And he laughed so
uproariously that the balls on the Christmas tree trembled
and jingled.

A square is not a circle, and a man is not an angel. Squares
seem to have resigned themselves to not being round. At any
rate nothing to the contrary has ever been heard. We may assume
that they agree to having their four right angles and their four
sides of equal length. They form the most perfect quadrilateral
that can be imagined. With this their ambition is satisfied.

With human beings it is different, at least with those who have
lofty aspirations. They do not want to become perfect human
beings, which would be a beautiful and appropriate goal; they
want to become angels. The imperfect Frau Lehmann does not
want to become the perfect Frau Lehmann; she wants to be a kind
of Saint Cecilia. Luckily she does not achieve this false aim. If she
did, Herr Lehmann and the children would find it no laughing
matter. A saint or an angel would not do for them, but a perfect
Frau Lehmann would. Yet this is just what they do not get,
because this is just what Frau Lehmann does not want to become.
And so in the end she looks like a rectangle gone askew from
trying to become a circle. And that is not a beautiful sight.

My mother was no angel, and did not want to be one. Her ideal
was more realistic. Her goal was distant, yet not up in the clouds.
It was attainable. And as she was more strong-minded than
anyone I've ever known and would not allow herself to be
dissuaded from anything by anyone, she achieved her aim. Ida
Kästner wanted to be a perfect mother to her boy. And because
she so much wanted to be that, she had no consideration for
anyone, not even for herself, and became the perfect mother. All

her love and imagination, all her industry, every moment of her time, her every thought – in fact her whole existence she staked, like a frenzied gambler, on one single card – on me! Her stake was her whole life to its last breath.

I was the card, so I simply had to win. I dared not disappoint her. That was why I became the best pupil in the school and the best-behaved son possible at home. I could not have borne it if she had lost her great game. Since she wanted to be and was the perfect mother, for me, her trump card, there seemed no choice but to become the perfect son. Did I become this? I certainly tried to. I had inherited her talents – her energy, her ambition and her intelligence. That was at least something to begin with. And when I, her sole capital and stake, sometimes felt really tired of always winning and of only winning, one thing and one thing only kept me going: I truly loved that perfect mother; I loved her very much indeed.

Attainable goals are particularly strenuous precisely because we want to attain them. They challenge us and, without looking to the right or to the left, we set out to achieve them. My mother looked neither to the right nor to the left. She loved me, and nobody else. She was kind to me, but that was the limit of her kindness. She treated me to her gaiety, and had none left for others. She thought only of me, she had no other thoughts. Her life and every breath she breathed were dedicated to me, only to me.

That was why everyone else found her cold, stern, haughty, domineering, intolerant and egotistical. She gave me everything she was and everything she had and for everyone else she was empty of heart and hands; proud and upright to be sure, yet a pitiable soul all the same. This filled her with sadness and made her profoundly unhappy, driving her many a time to the brink of despair. I do not say this lightly; I know what I am saying. For I was there when her eyes used to grow dark with trouble –

long ago, when I was a little boy. And when I came home from school I used to find those hurriedly scribbled notes lying on the kitchen table. 'I can't go on,' they said. Or, 'Don't look for me.' Or, 'Goodbye, my dear boy.' And the flat was empty and dead.

Then I ran through the streets towards the Elbe and the stone bridges, hunted and whipped on by wild fear, sobbing aloud and almost blinded by tears. My temples throbbed, my head buzzed, my heart pounded. I banged into the passers-by; they scolded me, and I raced on. I staggered for want of breath, sweated and froze, fell, picked myself up again, did not notice that I was bleeding, and raced on. Where could she be? Would I find her? Had she done it? Had she been rescued? Was there still time, or was it too late? 'Mamma! Mamma! Mamma!' I stammered without ceasing, and ran – for *her* life. 'Mamma! Mamma! Mamma!' I could think of nothing else. In this race with death it was my one unending prayer.

I found her almost every time. And almost every time on one of the bridges. There she stood, motionless, staring down at the river, and looking like a wax figure. 'Mamma! Mamma! Mamma!' I shouted louder and louder. With my last ounce of strength I dragged myself towards her. I took hold of her, tugged at her, threw my arms round her, shouting and crying and shaking her as if she were a big white-faced doll. And then she woke up as if she had been sleeping with her eyes open. Only then did she recognize me. Only then did she notice where we were. Only then was she frightened. Only then could she cry and clasp me to her, and murmur in a hoarse, broken voice, 'Come, my boy. Take me home.' And after the first faltering steps she whispered, 'It's all right again now.'

Sometimes I did not find her. Then I wandered desperately from one bridge to the other, ran home to see if she had come back in the meantime, ran back to the river, down the steps by the bridge and along the Neustadt Embankment, sobbing and trembling with fear lest I should find boats out, and men fishing with long grippers for someone who had jumped from the bridge. Then I dragged myself home again and threw myself on her bed, shaken with hope and despair. Half fainting with exhaustion I fell asleep. And when I awoke she was sitting beside me, and she clasped me in her arms. 'Where have you been?' I asked, joyful yet perplexed. She did not know. She shook her head. Then she tried to smile and whispered, this time too, 'It's all right again now.'

One afternoon, instead of going to play, I went secretly to Dr Zimmermann in his consulting room and poured out my heart to him. He twirled his turned-up moustaches between his tobacco-stained fingers, looked at me kindly and said: 'Your mother works too hard. Her nerves are not sound. These are crises, sharp and short like summer thunderstorms. They have to happen. It's Nature's way of righting itself again. The air is doubly fresh and pure afterwards.' I looked at him doubtingly. 'Human beings are part of nature too,' he said. 'But everyone doesn't want to jump from bridges,' I objected. 'No,' he said, 'fortunately not'.

He patted me on the head. 'Your mother should take a few months' rest, somewhere near – Tharant or Weixdorf, or Langebrück. You could go out there at midday from school and remain with her until evening. You could do your homework in Weixdorf just as well.' 'She won't do that,' I replied, 'on account of her customers. A few months, that would be too long.' 'Less wouldn't be much good,' he answered, 'but you're right – she won't do it.' 'It's because of me she won't do it,' I said guiltily. 'She's wearing herself out because of me. It's for me she needs the money.' As he took me to the door, he patted me on the shoulder. 'Don't reproach yourself for that. If she hadn't you, it would be much worse.'

'You won't tell her I was here, will you?' 'Now, what do you think? Of course not!' 'And you don't believe that she'll really … do it … perhaps … one day – from the bridge?' 'No,' he said, 'I don't think so. Even if she forgets everything around her, her heart will still think of you. You're her guardian angel.' And he smiled at me.

Often in the course of my life I have thought of those last words. They have comforted and oppressed me at the same time. I remembered them again when, as a man of about fifty, I visited my mother in a nursing home. Many terrible things had happened. Dresden lay in ruins, but my parents had survived the bombs. We had been separated for a long time. The postal service and the railways had been broken down for quite a while. Now at last we saw each other again – in a nursing home. For my mother, who was nearing eighty and worn out by a life of hardship and toil, was suffering from loss of memory and needed nursing and care.

She was holding a handkerchief on her knees and kept restlessly folding and unfolding it, as she looked at me, smiling but puzzled. She seemed to recognize me, nodded and then asked me, 'But where's Erich?' She asked me about her 'son! And my heart contracted, just as it did when she used to stand, distraught, on one of the bridges.

'Even if she forgets everything around her,' Dr Zimmermann had said, 'her heart will still think of you.' Now her eyes had forgotten even me, their only joy and goal. But only her eyes — not her heart.

12

UNCLE FRANZ BECOMES
A MILLIONAIRE

THE last chapter did not sound very cheerful. A child was troubled, and that child was myself. Perhaps I should not have told you about it? No, that would have been wrong of me. Trouble comes, I believe, just as hailstones and forest fires do. You can imagine a happier world than ours. A world in which no one is hungry and no one has to go away to war. But even then there would be plenty of trouble left, which neither wiser Governments nor stronger measures could do away with. And he who would deny that trouble exists would be a liar.

The world looks rosy if you look at it through rose-coloured spectacles. That may be a pretty sight, but it is an optical illusion. It is due to the spectacles, not to the world. The person who confuses the two will get a nasty shock when life lifts the spectacles off his nose.

There are also opticians – I really mean poets and philosophers – who sell people spectacles with black lenses. And when you look through these spectacles the world is a vale of tears, a hopelessly dark and gloomy planet. The person who recommends us dark glasses to keep the sun from dazzling our eyes is an honest shopkeeper. But the person who puts them on us to make us think the sun does not shine at all is a cheat.

Life is not all rosy nor all black but multicoloured. There are good people and bad people, and the good people are sometimes bad, and the bad people are often good. We laugh and we cry, and sometimes we cry as if we could never laugh again. Or we laugh as heartily as if we had never cried. We are happy and unhappy, and there is even happiness in the midst of adversity. Anyone who knows better is a know-all. If someone asserts that two and two make five, he is alone in his opinion and that is that. He can keep his originality. We don't want it. Old truths are not original and they do not sound original, but they are and remain truths. And that is what matters.

I had wept as if I could never laugh again; and yet I was able to laugh again just as if I had never wept. 'It's all right again now,' my mother had said. And so it was all right again — or almost.

Hecht Strasse was a narrow, drab, overcrowded street. Because the shops were cheap in it Uncle Franz and Uncle Paul had started here as young butchers. And although the two single-fronted shops stood opposite one another, separated only by the roadway, and the two owners were called Augustin, they got on well together. Both brothers were able, industrious, pleasant and popular. Their jackets and aprons were snow white, and their sausages, mince and brawn were excellent. Aunt Lina and Aunt Marie stood behind their respective counters from morning until evening and sometimes waved cheerfully across the street to one another.

Aunt Marie had four children, including Hans, who was blind from birth. He was always happy, enjoyed eating and laughing, and when his mother, my Aunt Marie, died he went into the Blind Institute. There he was trained in basket-making and piano-tuning, and when he was still very young Uncle Paul got a poor girl to marry him so that he would have someone to look after him. For the father himself had no time for his blind son.

The three former rabbit-dealers, including the eldest, Robert Augustin of Döbeln, were sturdy men. They didn't think much about themselves, and they didn't think of other people at all. They thought only of business. If the day were forty-eight hours long it might perhaps have been different. They might possibly have had a little time over for such unimportant trifles as their wives, children, brothers and sisters, or their own health.

But the day was only twenty-four hours long, so they were quite ruthless, even towards their own father. He suffered from asthma, had no money, and knew that he would soon die. But he was too proud to ask his three elder sons for help. He probably thought of the proverb that it is easier for a father to feed twelve children than for twelve children to feed a father.

The sisters in Döbeln, who were as poor as church mice, wrote to my mother and told her how bad things were with Grandfather. My mother went to the Hecht Strasse and implored her brother Franz to do something about it. He promised her he would, and he kept his word. He sent his father a few marks by money order and a picture postcard with hearty greetings and best wishes for his health. He didn't even write the card himself. He got his wife to do it for him. The son had no time to send a greeting to his father. But when the old man died shortly afterwards, Uncle Franz went to the funeral all right. He would not let it be said that he failed to do the proper thing.

These three brothers made an exception for weddings and silver weddings in the family, but above all for funerals. They found time for them. They turned up beside the coffin at the cemetery, dressed in their frock-coats and silk hats, with handkerchiefs for drying their tears. Their eyes and noses were red. And the tears were absolutely genuine.

They even sat down to table with the family afterwards. During the midday dinner the atmosphere was appropriately mournful. By the time the coffee and cakes came round there was laughter; and as they sipped their brandies afterwards the former rabbit-merchants were surreptitiously drawing their gold watches from their vest pockets. They were in a hurry to be off again. 'Goodbye!' 'Let us see you some time.' 'It's a pity we have to go, it was so pleasant here with you.'

It was only at their own funerals that they remained a little longer.

Franz and Paul Augustin continued to live in the Hecht Strasse even after they had sold their butchers' shops at a profit and become full-blown horsedealers at last. There was room enough

for stables in the backyards, indeed more than enough for Uncle Paul because he bought and sold only half-bred and thoroughbred horses, carriage and riding-horses, the finest of the fine. After only a few years he was able to style himself 'Supplier to Royalty'. He had the title painted under the firm's name over his front door. And now he was almost on the same footing as the Court Jeweller. The latter sold only the most beautiful gems and pearls; and Uncle Paul sold only the finest horses. For these he found ten stables sufficient. The King himself often came there. Just imagine! Into narrow, mucky Hecht Strasse, to my Uncle Paul. With the princes, and the Lord Chamberlain, and the Life Guards!

All the same, I visited the yard and stables on the other side of the street a hundred times oftener, and liked it there a thousand times better. Uncle Franz was as rude as a pig, and he was definitely not cut out to be a Supplier to Royalty. Heaven knows what he might not have said to King Friedrich August III of Saxony! He would probably have clapped him heartily on the back, and the Lord Chamberlain and aide-de-camp would at the very least have fainted with shock. But I liked my barbarously rude Uncle Franz very much better than my high and mighty Uncle Paul, who was nicknamed 'The Baron' by his brothers and sisters. And I felt at home among his stablemen and horses.

The brown wooden stalls which ran down each side of the narrow yard held about thirty horses – the Oldenburgs and Holsteins from Denmark and East Prussia, the mighty Brabants from Belgium with their broad cruppers and enormous light-coloured manes. The stable men carried in hundredweights of hay, oats and chopped feed, and gallons of fresh water – bucket after bucket of it. The horses ate and drank the most astonishing amount. They stamped their heavy hooves, swished the swarms of flies from their backs with their tails and neighed hearty greetings to each other from stable to stable. When I came near they turned their heads and regarded me with the strange patient gaze of their inscrutable eyes. Sometimes they nodded and sometimes they shook their enormous heads, but I did not know what they meant. Rasmus, the big gaunt head stableman from Denmark, who couldn't pronounce the letter s, walked from stable to stable examining them. And Uncle Bruno limped busily over the cobblestones beside the stout vet, who came often.

Horses have the same kind of illnesses as we have. Many of them, such as influenza and colic, have the same names. Others are called glanders, malanders, staggers and spavin, and they are all very dangerous. We do not die of a cough, a cold in the head, a sore throat, mumps or gripe. With those prehistoric vegetarians, horses, one can never be sure. If they eat grass that is too damp their stomachs blow out like balloons and pains cut like knives into their vitals, their intestines are contorted, and death knocks at the stable door. If they are sweating and gulp a lot of cold water, they begin to cough, their glands swell, their nostrils drip, they get feverish, their bronchial tubes begin wheezing, their eyes become dull, and again death raises his hand and knocks. Sometimes the vet came in time, but often he came too late. Then the knacker's cart rumbled into the yard and fetched away the corpse, for the skin, hooves and horsehair were all of use.

The worst thing about a horse's death was the loss of money, so the grief and mourning were not excessive. For after all the horses were not members of the family. They were more like four-legged hotel guests who spent a few days in Dresden with full board and lodging, then continued on their journey – to the estate of a nobleman, to a brewery, or to a barracks, as the case might be. Or, now and then, to the knacker's yard. Hotel-keepers do not weep when a guest dies. They just carry him privately down the back stairs.

Uncle Franz lived in an uncomfortable, tastelessly furnished flat over the butcher's shop in which another butcher had long since been cutting cutlets and flattening them out with the broad side of the chopper. Frieda, the silent and energetic maid who had come from the Erzgebirge as a young girl many years before, ruled over the flat. She did the cooking and washing and cleaning and was like a mother to my cousin Dora. For the mother herself, my Aunt Lina, had no time for her child.

Without any commercial education she had become office manager and sat in the office from morning until night. Uncle Franz had nothing to do with cheques, invoices, taxes, wages, bills of exchange, health insurance, bank accounts or similar trifles. He had said, 'You deal with those,' and she dealt with them. If he had said, 'Jump off the Church of the Holy Cross at six o'clock this evening,' she would have jumped from it. Possibly she would have left a note up in the tower: 'Dear Franz, please forgive me for being eight minutes late in jumping off, but I was delayed by the auditor. Your loving wife Lina.' Luckily the idea of making her do such a thing never entered his head. If it had, he would have lost his managing clerk, which would have been stupid of him; and my Uncle Franz was anything but stupid.

The office, or counting-house, as offices were called then, was on the ground floor of a small back building at the end of the yard, between the lines of stables. Here Aunt Lina served and reigned. Here, at her desk, she dealt with the tradespeople delivering goods. The stablemen came here for their weekly wages. Here she wrote out cheques and kept the books. Here the auditor examined her accounts. Against the wall behind her stood the safe, and she alone had the key to it. A bunch of keys and a money-bag dangled over her apron. She kept a pencil stuck slantwise into her hair. She was a strong-minded woman and would not take cheek from anyone. Only one person in the whole world seemed to awe her – the 'Master', as she called her husband when he was not there. When he was in the room or on the phone, she called him Franz – 'Yes, Franz.' 'Of course, Franz.' 'Certainly, Franz.' 'Naturally, Franz.' And her otherwise very domineering voice sounded like that of a schoolgirl.

When he wanted her he just roared 'Wife!' from wherever he was at the moment, and she instantly called back, 'Yes, Franz!' and ran as if her life depended on it. Then he had only to say, 'I'm starting for the Fair at Flensburg with Rasmus tonight. Give me twenty thousand marks in hundred-mark notes.' Still at a run she would pull off her apron, and an hour later she would be back from the bank with two hundred hundred-mark notes. Later, when they lived at the villa, I used to run instead of her. But my bank messenger period does not come in yet.

Uncle Franz's great time began after he had come back from the horse fairs and auctions and the horses had been unloaded on to the ramp of the Neustadt Goods Station and led along the Dammweg and over the Bischofs-Platz into Hecht Strasse by the stablemen hired for the journey. The horses had first to be fed up because the change of climate and the journey in the goods wagons had taken it out of them.

But a few days later the customers crowded into the yard as if to a fair. All of them were impressive people with fat notecases and a tremendous knowledge of horses. Officers with their sergeant-majors of cavalry, landowners, large farmers, directors of breweries, transport contractors, gentlemen from the Public Health Department of the Borough of Dresden and from Pfund's Dairy – the scene gave the impression that stout men were up for sale rather than horses. Uncle Bruno limped around from one to the other with a box of Havanas. Inquisitive women and children leaned out of the back windows of the surrounding houses, enjoying the drama and waiting for the star actor, Franz Augustin, the lord of the horses, to appear. And when he appeared, when he came in the gateway, smiling, with a cigar in his mouth, swinging his thick bamboo walking-stick, his brown bowler hat perched jauntily on one side of his head, even people who had never seen him before knew at once, 'There he is! He'll make me pay through the nose for that light chestnut gelding I fancy, but he'll make me feel he's making me a present of

the animal.' For no one could hold out against Uncle Franz's self-confident strength and gay cocksureness. The spot where he planted himself, debonair and four-square, after a bit of hand-shaking and back-slapping, automatically became the magnetic

centre, and all waited on his word and obeyed his commands –
the stablemen, the horses, and even the customers!

The horses were put through their paces one after the other.
The stablemen held them on a short rein, and ran up and down
the yard with them. Particularly intractable horses were paraded
by Rasmus. Even the most hard-mouthed crib-biter trotted
meekly as a lamb when led by him. Sometimes Uncle Franz
flicked his whip, but generally he only waved his big white
handkerchief. This he did like a variety artist. The handkerchief
fluttered like a flag in the wind and set even the dullest and
heaviest steeds in motion.

After a horse had shown its paces the would-be purchasers came
nearer and examined its teeth and fetlocks. Uncle named his price
and refused to allow lengthy bargaining. Then the purchase was
sealed by a resounding handslap. Even hearing it made my
palms smart. Aunt Lina drew the pencil from her hair and noted
the purchaser's name. But this was hardly necessary, for the
handslap had the force of an oath. Anyone who did not keep to

an agreement sealed in this way would have been finished as a businessman; and no one could afford that.

My uncle often brought back so many horses that more than half of them had to be boarded out in other people's stables — with his brother Paul or his friend, Councillor Gäbler. At such times the inspection and parading of the horses lasted for days on end and there were great goings-on in the public house in front of Uncle's premises. You could not have cut the cigar smoke with even garden shears. The noise and loud laughter could be heard right down the street. Uncle Franz drank like a fish but kept a clear head. Uncle Bruno was drunk as a lord after only four whiskies. And Aunt Lina did not drink at all but just kept on taking the cash silently and steadily. The fat notecases round about became visibly thinner as hundred-, five-hundred and thousand-mark notes came rolling in. Aunt scribbled receipts, then stuck

the indelible pencil into her hair again and took the bundles of
money down to the office safe at the bottom of the yard.

'Franz Augustin will have a breakdown before he's done,'
people said. Have a breakdown? Little they knew him! But they
did not mean it all that literally; secretly they were very proud of
him. Here was someone showing the world that you could
become a millionaire even in Hecht Strasse. They thought a lot
of him for that. To them his success was like a fairy-tale, and they
added to it as they went along. 'A person who has become so
rich must show off his riches. He should have a palace. He must
leave the Hecht Strasse. He owes that to the Hecht Strasse.'
'Nonsense,' growled Uncle Franz. 'Our flat over the butcher's
shop is good enough for me; and I'm hardly ever at home,

anyway.' But public opinion in Hecht Strasse was stronger than he; and finally he gave way...

He bought a house, No. 1 Anton Strasse. 'House' is hardly the right name for it. It was a spacious, two-storey, detached villa with a secluded garden almost like a little park, which stretched down to the Albert Platz, that same Albert Platz which I passed through on my way to school, a busy yet stately square containing the theatre and the two great fountains which were called respectively 'Silent Water' and 'Stormy Waves'.

With the big villa and its little park went great high trees, a greenhouse, two summer-houses, and outbuildings containing a stable and a coach-house with a coachman's flat over it. Frieda the perfect servant set up residence in the flat, and received the title of housekeeper. She was given a maid and a gardener to help her and she took over sole management of the household. From the very first day she coped with her new duties as if she had grown up in a large, detached residence. Aunt Lina found it more difficult. She did not want to be a fine lady, and she never became one. She and Frieda both came from the Erzgebirge and their fathers had been coal miners in the same pit.

13

THE VILLA ON THE ALBERT PLATZ

IT was only a stone's throw from No. 48 Königsbrücker Strasse
to No. 1 Anton Strasse, and as Aunt Lina felt like a fish out of
water in her villa she loved us to visit her. When the weather was
fine I used to go over there quite early in the afternoon. Uncle
was away, sitting in an express train somewhere or other. Aunt
was writing invoices and receipts at her desk in the Hecht Strasse.
My cousin Dora was visiting a school friend, and so I had the
house and garden to myself.

Most of all on such occasions I loved to sit on the garden wall
watching the comings and goings on the Albert Platz. The trams
to the Altstadt, to the White Hart, Neustadt Station, and Klotzsche
and Hellerau stopped right under my eyes as if specially for my
delight. Hundreds of people got in and out, and changed trams,
just to give me something to look at. Lorries, cabs, motor-cars
and pedestrians did what they could to entertain me. The two
fountains showed their skill in water-play. The fire-brigade
rattled past, with hooting of horns and clanging of bells. Perspiring
grenadiers marched back singing to their barracks from an
exercise. A royal carriage rolled elegantly past. At the corner,
ice-cream vendors dressed in white sold ices at five and ten
pfennigs. A cask rolled off a brewer's dray and an eager crowd

gathered. The Albert Platz was the stage; I was seated in a private box between the jasmine and the trees, and I never tired of the play.

After a time Frieda would tap me on the shoulder and say, 'I've left your coffee.' Then I would sit down in the shady, airy, wrought-iron arbour and take my afternoon coffee like a prince. After that I would inspect the currant bushes and cherry trees, or, if it was autumn, knock down nuts from the walnut tree with a long pole. Or I would run to fetch something for Frieda from the greengrocer's opposite – dill, lump sugar, onions, chives, pumpernickel, or the like. Near the shop, half hidden in its garden, was a little house with a tablet on the gate saying, GUSTAV NIERITZ LIVED AND DIED HERE. He was a teacher and school inspector who had written many, many books for children, all of which I had read. He had died in the little house in the Anton Strasse in 1876, no less famous than his Dresden contemporary Ludwig Richter, the artist and painter. People still love and admire Ludwig Richter but no one remembers Gustav Nieritz any longer. Time chooses what is to endure and last, and time is generally right.

We often walked over to the villa in the evening too, especially when Uncle Franz was away. At such times Aunt Lina felt so lonely, in spite of having Dora, that she was delighted when we came and took supper with her in the living-room. Frieda was an expert in making sandwiches and we should have offended her deeply if we had left so much as one liver sausage or ham sandwich. As no one wanted to offend her, we did our very best.

Those were very pleasant evenings. Over the sofa hung an exact copy of a picture from the Art Gallery. It showed an old coachman standing beside his horse, after lighting the harness lamp. The artist, Hofmann of Trachau, who was really an impressionist painter, had copied the picture in the Zwinger to make some money and Aunt Lina had bought it as a present for

Uncle Franz when they bought the house. 'A picture?' Uncle had said, wrinkling his nose. 'Well, if you like. At least it's got a horse in it.'

The evenings when Uncle was not away from home were less pleasant. Not that he was at home. Heaven forbid! He was sitting in inns and public houses, drinking 'beyond his thirst' with other men, making passes at the barmaids, and of course selling horses. But he could come in unexpectedly at any time, since nothing in the world is impossible. So we had to keep to the kitchen.

It was a beautiful and spacious kitchen. And why not? We kept our kitchen beautiful too. And Frieda's sandwiches tasted just as good here as in the living-room. But all the same it was not really comfortable. Infected by Aunt Lina's nervousness we all sat huddled round the kitchen table. The whole great house was empty, and Aunt Lina looked as if she were a visitor herself. We sat and ate with our ears laid back like rabbits. Would he come or not? It was uncertain. It was unlikely. But sometimes he did.

First we heard the garden gate slam, and Frieda said, 'The Master is coming!' Then the front door was flung open so violently that the multicoloured leaded panes tingled, and Aunt Lina, overwhelmed with a mixture of fear and joy, cried, 'The Master's here!' Then the single word 'Wife!' like the roar of a lion, came from the corridor. And with a cry of 'Yes, Franz,' Aunt, with Frieda and Dora behind her, rushed into the vestibule, where the lord of the horses was already impatiently holding out his hat and walking-stick for them to take. They took the articles deftly from his hands, then all three together helped him out of his coat, put stick, hat and coat into the hall cupboard, and ran ahead of him through the corridor to open the living-room door and turn on the light.

He sat on the sofa with a grunt and stretched out a leg. Aunt Lina knelt before him and drew off his shoe. Frieda knelt beside

her and fished his slippers from under the sofa. While Aunt pulled off the second shoe and Frieda pushed the first slipper over his foot, he growled the word 'Cigar!' Dora ran into the study, hurried back with a box of cigars, and matches, opened the box, laid it back on the table when he had taken a cigar and held a lighted match ready. When he had bitten off the end of the cigar and spat it out on the carpet, she gave him a light.

The three stood and knelt round him, hanging on his words and awaiting his further orders like slave-women round their Grand Mogul. At first he said nothing, so they had to keep hovering about him. He puffed his cigar, stroked his fair moustaches which

were already going slightly grey, and looked like a well-fed
robber. Then he asked: 'Any news?' and Aunt Lina delivered her
report. He grunted. 'Would you like something to eat?' asked
Frieda. 'I've already dined,' he snapped, 'with Gäbler in the
Bunch of Grapes.' 'Will you have a glass of wine?' asked his
daughter. 'I don't mind,' he said graciously, 'but be quick! I have
to go out again.' And off she dashed to the sideboard and the
wine-cellar.

Meantime we sat in the kitchen and kept quiet. My mother
smiled ironically, my father was cross, and I ate a sandwich now
and then. We knew by heart what was happening in the living-
room. It only remained to be seen which of the three possible
endings the comedy would have this evening.

Either Uncle Franz really went out again, the three slaves came
back to the kitchen, possibly with the opened bottle of wine,
and we stayed another hour or so. Or else Uncle remained at
home. In this case Frieda reappeared alone, and with a slightly
embarrassed air let us out of the back door. We slunk along the
gravel path as if we were burglars and trembled when the garden
gate creaked. The third ending of the comedy was the most
dramatic, and it happened not infrequently.

Sometimes Uncle would eye Aunt Lina suspiciously and ask
with assumed indifference, 'Is there anyone else in the house?'
Aunt Lina's nose became pale and pointed and her silence was an
answer in itself. Then he asked, 'Who? Out with it!' 'Oh, it's only
the Kästners,' she answered with a feeble smile. 'Where are
they?' he asked, leaning forward threateningly. 'I asked you
where are they?' 'They're in the kitchen, Franz.' Now the storm
broke loose. He was furious. 'In the kitchen!' he roared. 'It's only
the Kästners! You hide our relatives away in the kitchen? Have
you all gone daft, eh?' He stood up, stubbed out the butt of his
cigar on the table, groaned with rage, and stamped into the

corridor. Unfortunately he had his slippers on; with boots the scene would have been much more effective.

He wrenched open the kitchen door, looked us all up and down, planted his hands on his hips, took a deep breath, and roared, 'So you put up with this, do you?' My mother answered calmly and gently, 'We didn't want to disturb you, Franz.' With a single movement of the hand he swept aside her remark. 'Who says that my relatives disturb me? It's quite incredible!' Then he stretched out his arm imperiously like a Field Marshal sending the reserves into the firing line, 'Come into the living-room at once. Or must you have a written invitation first? Ida! Emil! Erich! Come along there. Hurry up!'

He stamped on ahead. We followed him hesitantly, like poor sinners going to the stake. 'Wife! Frieda! Dora!' he cried. 'Two bottles of wine! Cigars! Something to eat!' The three slaves hurried off. 'We have already had something to eat in the kitchen,' said my mother. 'Then you must eat again,' he shouted irritably. 'And now sit down. Here, Emil, have a cigar.' 'I have some myself, thank you,' my father would say. It was the same old game. 'Take one,' commanded my uncle, 'you don't have cigars like these every day.' 'Very well, if I may,' my father said, taking one gingerly from the proferred box.

When we were all sitting under the lamp and had been provided with food and drink, Uncle rubbed his hands and said contentedly, 'Now we'll have a really pleasant evening. Tuck in, my boy. Why, you're not eating anything!' Luckily I was able to eat more then than I can now, so I munched through one sandwich after another for the sake of peace. And Dora winked at me when she caught my eye. Frieda poured out wine for us. Uncle brought up the old rabbit-dealing days in Kleinpelsen, and said, as always, what a little telltale my mother had been. And the angrier she got, the more pleased he was. When he had brought her to boiling point he began to lose interest and started discussing business matters with Aunt Lina, until all of a sudden he stood up, yawned loudly and declared that he would go to bed now. 'Don't let me disturb you,' he boomed, and off he went. Sometimes he was much more downright, and would say, as cool as you please, 'Well, there you are. Now you can go.' My Uncle Franz was certainly a character, and he had nerves as tough as ropes.

As I was often about the villa and the garden in the daytime as well, I was inevitably sent on an occasional errand. I acquitted myself of the most varied tasks with my accustomed punctuality and reliability and so, at about ten years old, I became Aunt Lina's right hand – I might also say, her left foot. For she had become very bad on her feet from the long years of standing about in the butcher's shop and later in the stables and yard. She preferred sitting to walking and I therefore took on many jobs which are not usually entrusted to little boys. I took agreements to the notary public to be legally attested, and bills of exchange to be protested. And after the big horse sales I took the money to the bank.

I shall never forget the astonished expressions of the other customers when I went up to the counter at the local branch of the Dresden Bank, opened the big thick briefcase and took out the bundles of money which I had counted through with Aunt Lina. The cashier counted and counted and counted. He stuck printed strips of paper on to the bundles and made notes which I compared carefully with mine. Five thousand marks, ten thousand marks, fifteen thousand, twenty thousand, twenty-five thousand, thirty thousand, sometimes even forty thousand marks and more. The customers who stood behind and beside me waiting their turn forgot their impatience in their astonishment.

If the cashier got a different total on his docket, he knew at once who had gone wrong. He had, of course. My addition was always right, so he totted up again from the beginning. At last I went off proudly with the receipt and the empty briefcase.

My aunt complimented me, locked the receipt into her desk and gave me five marks, or sometimes even ten. And at other times, too, she dipped generously into her purse. She was always a dear kind woman, not only when she gave me money.

But one day, however often she checked over her accounts, she found herself two hundred marks short. Her arithmetic was right. The money was missing. It was nowhere. Nowhere? That was impossible. So where was it? And inevitably the question arose: Who had stolen the two hundred marks? Who was the thief? Who could it possibly be? Uncle Franz and Aunt Lina discussed the matter privately together, and first decided who it could not be. This process of elimination has been practised from time immemorial. In lucky cases the criminal remains uneliminated.

After brief deliberation it was decided that only two persons were possible – Meta the maid, and me. Meta, who was cross-examined first, swore by all that was dear to her that she had not done it; and as they believed her, Aunt had no alternative but to

question me next. The conversation was very brief. Before
my aunt had finished speaking I had fled. My mother listened
to my report and said, 'It's a pity. They used to be really nice
people.' And with this the matter was closed as far as we were
concerned.

A few days later my aunt happened to find the money in a
drawer. No doubt she had put it there herself and forgotten it in
the press of more important business. My cousin Dora was the
first envoy to ring at our door. She told us what had happened and
brought kind greetings from the family. 'It was not your fault,
Dora,' said my mother, 'but it will be best if you take yourself off.'
Next day the perfect Frieda appeared, and she too was very
quickly shown the door. The day after that, Aunt Lina came
groaning up the stairs, in spite of her varicose veins. 'You know I
like you, Lina,' said my mother, 'but I will no longer know anyone who could think my boy a thief.' Saying this, she shut the
door in Aunt Lina's face.

When one more day had elapsed a carriage drew up in front
of the house and Uncle Franz climbed out. He made sure of the
house number, disappeared into the entrance, and shortly afterwards stood, for the first time in his life, at the door of our flat.
'Well, I never!' exclaimed my mother. 'What do you want here?'
'To see where you live,' he boomed. 'Aren't you going to let me
in?' 'No,' said my mother. But he pushed her aside and walked in.
Again she tried to bar his way. 'Don't be a fool, Ida,' he growled,
abashed, and pushed her before him as if he were a steam-roller.

The conversation between the brother and sister, which took
place in Paul Schurig's room, was pretty loud. I sat in the kitchen
and listened to them shouting at each other. It was a passionate
duet of abuse in which my mother's excited voice took the lead
more and more. By the time Uncle departed he was mopping his
forehead with his big handkerchief, but he seemed relieved all the

same. At the door of our flat he stopped and said, 'You've got a nice little place here.' Then he went.

'He has apologized,' said my mother. 'He has begged us to forget the matter and come back soon.' She went to the kitchen window and leaned out. We watched Uncle down below as he climbed into the driver's seat, loosed the brake, picked up the reins, clucked with his tongue and drove off. 'What do you think?' asked my mother. 'Shall we forget it?' 'I think we should,' I answered. 'Very well,' she said. 'That will be best. After all, he is my brother.'

And so all was as it had been. Again I looked down on the Albert Platz from the garden wall, took my afternoon coffee in the little summer-house, and carried a lot of money to the bank. The briefcase in which I carried the bills of exchange became fatter and fatter, and the old gardener said to me: 'I'd like to know what he's getting out of it. He can't eat more than one cutlet, and he can't put more than one hat on his head. And he won't be able to spend any money in his coffin. The worms will eat him gratis and for nothing.' 'It's ambition,' I ventured. The gardener made a face, 'Ambition! The man only comes home to sleep. He doesn't even know he's got a garden. He hasn't taken a day's holiday in his whole life. He won't give himself any rest until he's lying in the ground and looking at the radishes from underneath.' 'You talk rather a lot about death,' I remarked. He threw his cigarette end into the flower bed, gave it a clout with the spade and said: 'That's not surprising. I started life as a cemetery attendant.'

Of course he was right. The life that Uncle Franz and Aunt Lina lived was quite crazy. They hardly had time to breathe. They never found any time to look at the flowers in their own garden. They became richer and richer. But what did they get out of it? Once the doctor sent Aunt Lina to Bad Elster to take a cure. After ten days she was back again. She had not had a moment's peace. Even in her dreams she had been thinking of sick horses and bills of exchange gone wrong. When Dora had holidays she went travelling and hiking with Mother and me, and Uncle thought even that unnecessary. 'What's all this newfangled nonsense?' he asked crossly. 'Did we go to the seaside when we were children?' And when Dora was fifteen and it was decided to send her to a boarding school, he didn't send her to Lausanne or Geneva or Grenoble. He sent her to the Boarding School for Young Ladies run by the Moravian Sisters at Herrenhut, Saxony, and it was such a strict and pious institution that the poor girl came back quite pale, nervous and broken-spirited.

When she was twenty she married a businessman whom Uncle approved of, and she died giving birth to her first child. It was a boy. He was christened Franz and was brought up by Uncle Franz and Aunt Lina. They lost all their money in the inflation, but Uncle Franz would not be beaten. He got the family fortunes on their feet again, and then it was all up with him. He collapsed suddenly like a felled tree, and died. But he left enough money to enable Aunt Lina to go on living at the villa and bring up their grandson, with Frieda's help. And she gave him a most careful upbringing, that grandson whose fair hair and blue eyes reminded her to the end of her days of her Dora.

Or rather, not to the end of her days but of his, for he was killed in 1945 on the retreat from Hungary, shortly before the collapse of Germany. He was a medical student and was serving in the Army as a medical auxiliary. He left a young wife and a little fair-haired, blue-eyed boy who now reminded my aunt of two pairs of blue eyes which were closed for ever. Then Aunt Lina herself died.

Would it have been any use if a fellow-passenger had said to Uncle Franz one night, about the year 1910, as he sat in an express train going to Holland: 'Forgive me for disturbing you, Herr Augustin, but I am the Archangel Michael, and I have been sent to tell you that you are absolutely on the wrong track.' Would it have been any use? 'Kindly leave me alone!,' Uncle Franz would have growled. And if the person opposite him had repeated emphatically that his message was important and that he really was the Archangel Michael, Uncle would have merely pushed his bowler hat down over his eyes and said, 'For all I care your name may be Hare!'

14

THE TWO FACES OF HERR LEHMANN

AFTER the first four years of school about half my fellow-pupils left Tieck Strasse and proudly re-emerged after Easter wearing caps of many colours, in the first forms of the various secondary schools. They were not the better half, but even the most stupid among them thought they were. And we others, though left behind in Tieck Strasse, were not behind intellectually. We were all of us aware that the question 'Secondary school or not?' had been answered, not by ourselves but by the parental purse. It was an answer from the wrong quarter, and it could not fail to leave a touch of bitterness in many a child's heart. Life was unjust, and it did not even wait until after we were confirmed to show us that.

Because many boys from parallel classes had wandered out into the land of the coloured school-caps, the two remnants of classes left were amalgamated to form a single class. And our form master, whose frightful reputation had preceded him, was a teacher named Lehmann. We had been told that boys were made to learn more in one year with him than in two years with other teachers, and we soon perceived that this report was not exaggerated. People had also told us that he broke a cane a week, and this story too was more or less true. He had made us tremble before we knew him, and we trembled still more when we got to know him. His rule made both our heads and tails ache.

Herr Lehmann made no jokes and understood no jokes. He loaded us with so much home-work that we sank under the weight. He harried us with so many things to learn, so much dictation and so many other tests, that even the brightest and best pupils became nervous. When he walked into the classroom and said in his cold-blooded way: 'Take out your copybooks,' we felt we would like to crawl into the nearest mousehole. Only there wasn't one there, at least not for thirty boys. And the story that he wore out a cane a week was only half correct — he wore out two.

Our Herr Lehmann was addicted to regular daily outbursts of anger. His anger got the better of him at the sight of lazy pupils, cheeky pupils, stupid pupils, silent pupils, cowardly pupils, stubborn pupils, whispering pupils, tearful pupils, despairing pupils. And which of us was not one or the other at one time or another? Herr Lehmann's anger had a choice of pretexts.

He boxed our ears until our cheeks swelled up. He took his cane, made us put out our hands, and struck us five or ten times on our open palms until they were red as fire, swelled up like newly risen dough, and smarted abominably. And then, since even as a child one is equipped with two hands, the other hand got its turn. If a boy kept his hand shut out of fear, he caned his knuckles and fingers. He ordered half a dozen boys to lean over the front bench side by side and he thrashed the six tautly stretched pant seats in quick succession until a distressful six-voiced boys' choir rent the air and the rest of us put our hands to our ears. When a boy standing at the blackboard did not know what to write, he caned the calves of his legs and behind his knees, and if the pupil turned round he fared even worse. Sometimes the cane split lengthwise; sometimes it broke across, and the bits whistled through the air and round our heads. When this happened he contented himself with boxes on the ear until the break. His hands

did not break in pieces; and when the next class began he produced
a new cane.

In those days there were teachers who took the same pleasure
in choosing their canes at the school porter's store that fastidious
smokers take in choosing their cigars. There were some who
soaked the cane in the wash-basin before use because it then hurt
twice as much. These were scoundrels who found an exquisite
pleasure in thrashing. Herr Lehmann was not of this crude and
common sort. He was less ordinary but much more dangerous.
He did not beat us because he enjoyed our pain. He beat us in
despair. He did not understand that we did not understand what
he understood. He could not grasp that we could not grasp him.
This made him beside himself. This made him lose his head and
his nerve and hit out all round like a madman. In fact, that school
was like a madhouse at times.

Again and again parents went to the headmaster and complained of him, with threats and tears. They brought medical
certificates testifying to the physical and mental harm their boys
had suffered. They threatened to go to law and claim compensation. The headmaster wrung his hands. Yes, he knew all that, he
said, and he had known it longer than we and our parents had
known it. And he promised to take the matter up with his colleague. But every time he ended with the same words: 'It's
terrible, because he is really my best teacher.' But of course that
was not true.

Herr Lehmann was a competent, diligent, clever man, and he
was trying to make us competent, diligent and clever pupils. His
aim was excellent; his way of going about it was atrocious. That
competent, diligent, clever man was not a good teacher. In fact,
he was not a teacher at all, for he lacked the most important virtue
of the educator – namely, patience. I do not mean that kind of
patience closely akin to apathy which makes people inclined to
jog along in a groove. I mean true patience, which is made up of

understanding, a sense of humour, and perseverance. He was no teacher. He was an animal tamer with pistol and whip. And he turned the classroom into a cage of wild beasts.

When he was not standing in the cage before thirty lazy, cowed, rebellious young animals he was an absolutely different person. The real Herr Lehmann came to light then, and one day I became acquainted with him – one whole long day.

At the time it was already clear that three of his pupils, Johannes Müller, my friend Hans Ludewig, and myself, were destined to escape from the uncomfortable cane a whole year before confirmation. We had passed with honours the entrance examination for the preparatory class of the teachers' training college. The professors had publicly expressed astonishment at our learning. Of course, they did not know the animal tamer to whom we owed our skill, so their praise went to the wrong quarter – to the pupils instead of to the stern disciplinarian. However, he too seemed proud of the result, and from that time onwards his cane made a wide detour round the three of us.

One day during the mid-morning break, he came up to me in the playground and asked casually, 'Would you like to come to the Sächsische Schweiz with me on Sunday?' I was flabbergasted. 'We'll be back in the evening,' he went on. 'Give your parents my compliments and ask their permission. We shall meet at eight o'clock sharp under the dome in the main station.' 'I'd love to,' I stammered. 'And bring your gym shoes with you.' 'My gym shoes?' 'We'll do a bit of climbing.' 'Climbing?' 'Yes, in the rocks. It's not dangerous.' He nodded and went off, munching his sandwich. The children fell back before him as if he were an ice-breaker. 'What did he want?' asked my friend Ludewig. And when I told him he shook his head. 'That's a good one,' he said. 'Gym shoes in your rucksack and the cane in his!'

★

Have any of you ever climbed one of those almost vertical sandstone rocks? Pressed close like a fly climbing up a wall, sticking your fingers and toes into the crevices, feeling above you for the next little ledges; as soon as the left hand has found a new hold, drawing the left foot up after it, repeating the manœuvre with the right hand and right foot, step by step, higher and higher, thirty or forty-five feet up until at last a ledge of rock offers you space and time to get your second wind? And then, in the same calm and cautious way, up the next vertical wall of rock? Have you ever tried anything like that yet? I warn the curious to leave it alone!

We rested on the narrow summit, to which a little crooked fir

tree had clung fast. The Valley of the Elbe shimmered in the summer haze. Weird ghostly rocks, cyclops with giants' heads, stood like sentries between us and the horizon. The air smelled of heat. Our boots, jackets and rucksacks lay somewhere down in the valley. We would have to get back to them, I thought, and I felt terribly sorry for myself.

True, Herr Lehmann was a master in the art of climbing – a fact I had not known before – and knew the local rocks inside out like the palm of his hand. He had shouted instructions to me and a couple of times had roped me to him. Yet, apart from one pleasant stretch at the mouth of a ravine, I could find nothing at all attractive in his rock-face climbing in God's free nature. I had found my fear anything but enjoyable; and even the view from the summit, glorious though it was, left me cold, because I was secretly dreading the way back and wondering if it would be even more difficult than the ascent. I was right.

Flies are better off than we are, at least on vertical walls, because when climbing downwards they climb head first. A man cannot do that. On vertical walls he has to keep head upwards even when climbing down. His whole attention is concentrated on his feet, which grope blindly downwards, inch by inch, feeling for the next hold. Then, if this next narrow ledge of porous weathered sandstone crumbles under his shoe and his foot is left hanging in mid-air, his heart simply stands still, luckily only for an instant. At such moments the climber is in grave danger of lowering his head because his eyes want to help his toes to search. This practice is not to be recommended.

To this day I remember my feelings as I looked down the wall of rock. Directly below us I saw our jackets and rucksacks lying, tiny as dolls' toys, by a roadway thin as a thread, and I shut my eyes tight in terror. I felt dizzy. There was a rushing sound in my ears. My heart stood still. At last it remembered its old task and began to beat again. That I finally arrived alive beside our rucksacks is obvious, since I am at this moment writing about it. But to assert that my life hung on a thread would not be quite correct. There was no thread there.

When we had put on our boots and jackets again at the foot of the rock, Herr Lehmann pointed out on a map the peaks he had not yet climbed. Their number was negligible. It was too dangerous to climb those, he said, and one must not risk one's life. We shouldered our rucksacks. 'And do you always go hiking alone at other times?' I asked. He tried to smile, but it was not all that easy as he had had no real practice. 'Yes,' he said, 'I'm a solitary wanderer.'

The afternoon passed more pleasantly. The gym shoes remained in our rucksacks. The rocks were no longer gymnastic apparatus but antediluvian remains of the Stone Age, bizarre witnesses to the fact that we were wandering over a former sea bed which had come to the surface thousands and thousands of years ago. The impressions of mussel shells in the sandstone told us this. The rocks had thrilling stories to tell of water, ice and fire, and Herr Lehmann knew how to listen to them. He understood the dialects of the birds. He studied the tracks of wild creatures. He showed me the spore-cells of the mosses, with their little peaked caps which later fall off. He knew the grasses by name, and as we ate our afternoon snack in a meadow we admired the infinite variety of their greens, and the delicate grassheads. Nature was an open book to him, and he read it aloud to me.

Then, as we travelled home in comfort on the deck of the paddle-steamer which had come sailing down from Bodenbach-Tetschen, he turned the pages of history for me. He told of the land of Bohemia, where our steamer had been anchored an hour ago, of King Ottokar, and Charles IV, of the Hussites and the unhappy wars of religion; of the disastrous and implacable rivalry between Prussia and Austria; of the Young Czechs, and of the collapse of the Austrian monarchy which was then threatening. Again and again, he said sorrowfully, Europe was trying to commit suicide. Those who could read the signs of the times were abused as know-alls, and so Europe's insane plan of self-destruction would succeed one day. He pointed to Dresden whose towers,

shining golden in the evening sun, were just coming into sight. 'There lies Europe,' he said gently.

As I thanked him on the Augustus Brücke for the pleasant day, he tried once more to smile, and this time he almost succeeded. 'I should have made quite a good private tutor,' he said, 'a tutor and travelling escort for three or four children. I would have been able to cope with them. But thirty pupils – that's twenty-five too many for me.' Saying this, he turned away. I looked after him.

Suddenly he stopped and turned back. 'This climbing excursion was a great mistake,' he said. 'I was more afraid for you than you were for yourself.' 'But it was a lovely day all the same, Herr Lehmann,' I replied. 'Then that's all right, my boy.' And now the solitary wanderer really went. He walked alone, he lived alone, he spent his leisure alone. And he had twenty-five pupils too many.

15

MY MOTHER – ON LAND AND IN WATER

ONCE more – since we have just been talking about rocks and rivers and meadows – I will put my trumpet to my lips and blow a fanfare in praise of my mother which will rend the air and echo from the mountains. From every direction of the compass the echo answers until it sounds as though a hundred bugles and trumpets were joining in my canticle of praise of Frau Kästner. And the brooks and waterfalls mingle in the concert, the geese on the village greens, the anvils before the smithies, the bees in the clover, the cows on the hillsides, the mill-wheels and the sawmills, the thunder over the valley, the cocks on dunghills and on church towers and the beer cocks in the inns where we used to spend the night. The ducks in the ponds quack their applause, the frogs croak 'Bravo!' and the cuckoo calls 'Cuckoo' from afar. Even the horses before the plough look up from their work and wish godspeed with a hearty neigh to the incongruous-looking pair on the highroad.

Who are these two singing, sun-tanned, cross-country hikers who drink from the gurgling streams like journeymen-artisans; who sit down to rest high on hills overlooking the valleys, eat a lunch of hard-boiled eggs, and for dessert feast their eyes on the glorious panorama; who wander stubbornly and tirelessly through the woods, clad in waterproofs and hoods, undeterred by storms and rain; who sup hot soup in the evening at the inn table and soon afterwards sink, gloriously tired, into the big farmhouse bed with its patchwork quilt?

For my sake hiking became Frau Kästner's joy, and her pursuit of this pleasure, so beneficial to health and spirits, was highly systematic. To begin with, when I was about eight years old, she ordered, to the astonishment of the tailoress, a weatherproof costume of coarse green frieze. It would have been cheaper ready-made, but such costumes were not to be found in the shops. Women did not go hiking in those days. It was very definitely not done. In accordance with the fashion of the times the skirt reached almost to the ankles! Then Frau Wähner the milliner made, to my mother's specification, a broad-brimmed green frieze hat which was firmly anchored and moored to the coiffure with two fork-shaped patent hatpins. And Frau Wähner, too, was astonished. Two green waterproof cloaks were next bought, while in his cellar workshop my father, who had long since forgotten how to be astonished, worked with fiery zeal on two indestructible green rucksacks, the smaller one for me. And so we were soon fitted out as greenly and as practically as possible.

Nothing was lacking. Everything necessary had been procured – two iron-tipped alpenstocks, a Thermos flask, containers for butter, sausages, eggs, salt, sugar and pepper, a saucepan for heating Maggi soups and Knorr's pease-porridge, a spirit-stove, and two light knives and forks. There was a box of leather-dressing for our stout boots, and only once did we mistake it for butter. It was somewhere in the Lausitz Mountains, but after the first bite we realized that leather-dressing is not to be recommended as a substance for spreading on bread. They say there is no accounting for tastes but as regards the edibility of leather-dressing there is really only one answer. At any rate that is my confirmed opinion since then and I resolutely reject all opinions to the contrary.

We were now fully equipped for hiking and only needed to learn hiking itself. Our hiking years were years of apprenticeship. In the beginning we believed, for instance, that even at a cross roads one knows instinctively the right road to one's destination. But when we arrived repeatedly, after four or sometimes even five hours' tramp, right back at the place from which we had started out in the morning, we began to doubt the instinct of the European. We were no Indians, and it was no help to try to steer our course by the sun, especially when we could not see it for woods or clouds.

So we took to looking up distant places on maps, and in the course of time we arrived at almost infallible results. Blisters on the feet, breathlessness and backache were also overcome quite early on. We were not discouraged by our initial failures, but continued to step out bravely, and eventually we came to know all the tricks of the seasoned hiker. We covered fifteen and sometimes even twenty miles a day without over-exertion, and in this way we wandered through Thuringia, Saxony, Bohemia and parts of Silesia. Taking our time, we climbed mountains over three thousand feet high, and we would have climbed even higher ones if there had been any around. When we came to a place which pleased us particularly we treated ourselves to a day's rest and lazed like purring cats. Then off we went again, marching in step, for a week or a fortnight, sometimes with my cousin Dora but more often and preferably without her. Our route-marches became pleasant promenades to our well-trained feet. There was no longer any trouble between us and nature. The rivers, the wind, the clouds, kept step with us. It was glorious, and it was healthy too. From head to foot and from foot to head we were *mens sana in corpore sano*, as we Latinists say.

In this way we explored the Thüringer Wald and the Lausitz Mountains, the Sächsische Schweiz and the Mittelgebirge in Bohemia, the Erzgebirge and the Isargebirge, and as we hiked we sang. We climbed all the peaks, big and little, from the Jeschken to the Fichtelberg and from the Rosstrappe to the Milleschauer. We solemnly inspected all the ruins and monasteries, fortresses and museums, cathedrals and castles, pilgrimage churches and rococo gardens which lay on our route. Then we went on, up and down the country, the lady hairdresser in the green frieze suit and her boy. Sometimes I had my gaily beribboned guitar with me and our singing went even better then. Herr von Eichendorff, who wrote some of the songs we sang, would have delighted in us if he had not happened to be dead. He could hardly have found two happier grandchildren of the Romantic period.

One day a gentleman who was still alive seemed to think something of the kind. After several days' hiking in the Sächsische Schweiz my mother and I had turned into the Linckescher Bad, a garden inn on the Elbe which had been made famous by E. T. A. Hoffmann, a romantic contemporary of Eichendorff. Königsbrücker Strasse was only round the corner, but we were thirsty and in no great hurry to get home. So we were taking our time over iced lemonade and, after the waitress had taken our money, we burst out laughing. For we had just discovered that we had only one single pfennig left between us!

The gentleman at the next table asked why we were so merry, and when we told him he made my mother an offer of marriage. He was, so he told us, a German who had made a fortune in the United States, and he was now looking for a wife to take back with him. He had noticed at once that my mother was the right woman for him and the fact that he would get such an intelligent and merry little son thrown in with her, so to speak, was an incomparable piece of good luck. Our irrepressible and increasing amusement only fired his eagerness instead of damping it. He was not in the least put off by the fact that we were already provided with a husband and father. An obstacle like that could be easily settled by money and mutual goodwill, he asserted. As nothing would dissuade him from his intention of marrying us both and taking us to America with him, there was nothing for it but to flee. As seasoned hikers we were nimbler on our feet than he was, so he lost sight of us. We were thus able to get out of reach in time and remain in Germany.

If my mother and I had not been able to walk so quickly that time, I might possibly be an American writer today or, in view of the fact that I knew German from childhood, I might be general representative for Coca-Cola, Chrysler cars or Paramount Films in the Province of Rhineland and Westphalia, or in Bavaria. And I should not have had to stand in a sentry-box in front of the above-mentioned inn, the Linckescher Bad, doing sentry duty in 1917. I might have been an American soldier instead. For there is nowhere left in this crazy world, however fast and far one travels, where one cannot be made a soldier against one's will. However, that does not belong here!

My father was if anything a more particular housewife than my mother. Before she and I came home from the wilds he began literally to wallow in soapsuds and polishes. He simply went berserk throughout the flat with scrubbing-brush and pail, brushes, polishers, floorcloths and window leathers. He hunted down every speck of dust, and banged and slammed away until late into the night. For of course he was in the suitcase factory all day and had no time for titivating the house until night. The

Grützners and the Stefans, who lived on the same floor, could not get a wink of sleep and said, 'Aha! The two hikers must be coming back tomorrow.'

It was the same every time. As soon as we stepped into the hall we felt much dustier and dirtier than we really were. The door-handles, the hearth, and the heating-stove doors were gleaming. The windows shone. We could have seen ourselves in the lino if we had wanted to. But we didn't want to. We knew already that we looked like tramps. There was only one remedy – a bath.

As soon as we looked more or less like decent city dwellers again I trotted through the streets heralding the good news that the hairdresser Ida Kästner was back from her holidays and was panting for female scalps. So for the next few days the waving, massaging, shampooing and setting went on non-stop until all the shopkeepers' wives and all the shop-girls behind their counters looked trim and neat again. They remained faithful to their hair-dresser. On one occasion a wedding was actually postponed because we were away hiking. The bride, an assistant at the Co-operative Stores, had insisted on this.

In the evening my father put his bike away in the cellar and came into the kitchen saying joyfully, 'So you're back again, are you!' He said no more; it was unnecessary. We did the talking!

Out of consideration for Mother's customers our walking tours did not last more than two weeks. But my summer holidays were longer than that, so we spent half and sometimes whole days of the remainder of them by the woodland lakes in the neighbour-hood of Dresden or in the King August-Friedrich Open-air Swimming Baths in Klotzsche-Königswald. Although I had failed miserably to learn swimming from the instructor who had me on a line, or from crawling about like a crab with a cork lifebelt round my middle, I had managed to become a fairly good swimmer by secretly practising and teaching myself.

As my mother found it hard to endure watching helplessly from the bank or the non-swimmers' pool when she could see nothing but my hair above water, she decided to learn to swim herself. Do you know what women's bathing-costumes looked like in those days? If not, count yourself lucky! They were like linen potato-sacks except that they were of bright colours and had long trouser-legs. And instead of close-fitting bathing-caps, ladies wore things like ruched chef's caps of red rubber. It was a sight to make the angels weep.

In this ludicrous and uncomfortable costume my mother entered the Weixdorfer Lake, lay flat on the surface of the water, made some energetic movements, opened her mouth to say something, and sank! What she wanted to say I do not know. It was certainly not what she actually did say when she emerged furiously a few seconds later. Filial piety and decency both forbid me to repeat her remarks. Posterity will be able to imagine more or less what they were. And as we know, posterity is always right. It is certain, however, that the unrepeatable declaration was made only after my mother had spat out a considerable quantity of the idyllically situated woodland lake, and tottered to the bank, leaning heavily on me.

She made no further attempts to become a swimmer. The element had refused to obey her, and it had to take the consequences. Everyone who knew my mother realized this. She had already learned to cope with quite different elements in her life. If water refused to co-operate with her, Ida Kästner was having nothing more to do with it.

Besides the royal cubicle surmounted by the Saxon crown, which was seldom used by royalty and was made available to non-royal persons for a trifling fee when the baths were crowded, there was another focal point of interest for many years at the King Friedrich-August Swimming Baths. It was a gentleman named Müller, who, despite his name, hailed from Sweden, and was the inventor of a system of open-air gymnastics which he had called 'Müllering' in his own honour. Herr Müller wore a small black moustache and a small pair of white bathing-trunks. He was tall and athletic and bronzed all over and if he were alive today he would definitely be elected Mr Universe as the acme of male beauty.

Herr Müller was beyond question the handsomest man of the new century. He thought so himself, in spite of his Scandinavian modesty. The Gentlemen's Bath – for the baths were strictly separated and a boy could only meet his mother in the restaurant – the Gentlemen's Bath heartily endorsed Herr Müller's opinion of Herr Müller, and as open-air gymnastics seemed to be conducive to manly beauty, we men 'müllered' enthusiastically and hopefully. Here's a picture of us, ranged one behind the other, in our bathing-trunks. Herr Müller brings up the rear. I am in front, almost as handsome as the Swede already, only minus a moustache and considerably smaller.

It goes without saying that the Ladies' Bath did not lag behind us in admiration. Thanks to his privileged position as inventor

and gymnastics master, Herr Müller was the only man permitted
to enter the paradise of the ladies, and the female population of
Dresden, shrouded in their 'open-air shirts', as they were called,
müllered so energetically that the lawns trembled. Yet the Swede
remained as handsome as ever, and when he could tear himself
away from the mothers and daughters of Eve he müllered with us
men to recuperate.

My mother had given up all thought of swimming, but she
acquired the art of cycling all right. Aunt Lina had given Dora a
bicycle. I had learned to ride on Father's, and as we thought we
could vary our holiday programmes still more by occasional
cycling tours, my mother bought herself a brand-new bicycle
from Seidel & Naumann's and mounted it with eager curiosity.
My father held the saddle firmly and ran alongside his veering
spouse, panting out instructions. These efforts were accompanied
not only by him but also by success, and now there was nothing
to stand in the way of our starting cycling excursions. He lent me
his bicycle, screwed the saddle down as low as possible, and
wished us good luck.

One can always do with luck. Level stretches and slight
gradients offered no difficulties worth mentioning, and as the
road went steeply uphill from Mordgrund Brücke to the White
Hart, we pushed our bikes. Then we mounted again, pedalled
along to Bühlau, and turned towards the heath. For we wanted to
have coffee in the Ullersdorfer Mill, with cheese-cakes or perhaps
Eierschecke, a cake peculiar to Saxony which, alas for humanity,
has remained unknown throughout the rest of the world. Or
perhaps we would have both, *Eierschecke* and cheese-cakes. And
that is exactly what we did have, only Mother could not share the
treat and drank only camomile tea. Opposite the Mill she had
tumbled against a garden wall in the village, and both wall and
daredevil cyclist had been slightly injured. The shock was greater

than the hurt, but her desire for coffee and cakes had vanished. On coming downhill she had forgotten to step on the back-pedalling brake, and for this she blamed both herself and the brake.

What had seemed at first to be simply bad luck, mischance or a beginner's awkwardness, proved in the course of time to be a law of her nature. My mother forgot the back-pedalling brake every time. As soon as we came to a gradient she tore along somewhat like the racing cyclists of the Tour de France when they are coming down from the Pyrenees. Dora and I scorched after her, and when we caught up on her at last at the foot of the hill we found her standing by her bicycle, pale with fright. 'I forgot again,' she would say. It was dangerous to life and limb.

Dora's heart and mine simply stood still as she shot down the steep road from the Augustusburg to Erdmannsdorf. Once again nothing collided with her. Perhaps her guardian angel had been riding tandem with her. But our cycling tours became more and more terror tours. It was enough to give us nightmares. Sometimes she jumped off half way down a hill and let the bicycle fall. At other times she deliberately turned it into the roadside ditch and fell herself. She always came off unscathed, but her nerves and ours were becoming more and more frayed. There was no sense in holidays like these, so we dismounted from our bicycles for ever and mounted Shanks's pony instead. The lady's bicycle found its way to the cellar and we found our way on foot as before where there was no back-pedalling brake to forget.

If I were a modern psychiatrist I should ponder the matter deeply and then publish in a psychological journal a paper entitled 'The Back-Pedalling Brake as Complex: An Interpretation', in which I should say something like this: 'To the above-named patient, Frau Ida K., there existed only an uphill course in life in general and cycling in particular. The opposite concept, namely, the downhill course, was utterly foreign to the aims and nature of her inexhaustible ambition, which sought in her promising son a compensation for her own frustrations. Since Ida K. categorically rejected the downhill course and was therefore incapable of considering its consequences, she naturally lacked all understanding of the precautionary measures necessary. If she nevertheless found herself confronted with a downhill course, on a cycling tour for example, her conscious mind refused to apply the rules which she had learned. These were automatically forced over the threshold of the conscious into the subconscious. There, in spite of the fact that excellent back-pedalling brakes are provided by bicycle manufacturers, this gadget passed an existence of which Frau Ida K. remained oblivious in moments of danger, precisely because it had been eradicated from her conscious mind. She was fundamentally incapable of taking cognizance either of the phenomenon of the downhill course or of any techniques whatsoever designed to counteract it. To have done so would have been implicitly to criticize and cast doubt upon her own invincible will to aspire. This was out of the question. She rather chose to doubt the principle that hills go down as well as up. In fine, she preferred, at whatever risk, to ignore reality.'

Fortunately I am not a professional diver into the depths of souls and so I may as well spare myself such probings and dissertations. I am much more interested in describing people than in explaining them. Description is explanation enough. All the same there may be a spark of truth in the above paragraph even though I wrote it only in jest. I shouldn't be at all surprised.

It is quite certain, at any rate, that we were all more than glad when those terrifying outings came to an end, and, what was more, to a lucky end. My father was the best pleased of all, for now he had his bicycle back and no longer had to take the tram to the factory during school holidays.

16

THE YEAR 1914

I WAS growing older, and my mother was not getting any younger. My cousin Dora left school and I entered the awkward adolescent stage. She began to wear her hair up and I began to look down on the short-legged female tribe. Dora kept to her new hairstyle, whereas I dropped my new attitude. But for a couple of years we were like strangers.

It was only later, when I was no longer a little boy, that we renewed our friendship. That was the time when she sportingly helped me to disguise myself as a girl. I wanted to play a trick on my professors and fellow-students during a party at the teachers' training college, and the joke came off splendidly. Never again have I met with such ardent attention and admiration as in that festively decorated gynmasium when I was posing as a young girl. Only when I made a run at the high horizontal bar, with my blond braids and padded-out blouse, and turned a somersault so that my skirt flew up, did the ardour cool off. But that doesn't belong here!

When Dora had been confirmed, as Aunt Lina had no time to look after her herself, my mother was engaged as her travelling-companion and chaperone, and she took her niece to the Baltic Coast for several holidays. The resort was called Müritz and they sent us a lot of picture postcards and also snapshots taken by the beach photographers.

During those motherless weeks I spent the hours out of school in the villa in the Albert Platz. In the evening my father came on his bicycle from the factory and joined me there. We had supper in the kitchen with Frieda and Aunt Lina and did not go home until we got the hint. Uncle Franz remarked laconically that his daughter's and sister's gallivanting to the Baltic Coast was fantastic nonsense, but Aunt Lina did not give in. She would never have plucked up so much courage on her own account, but she could be brave, within limits, for Dora.

Our lodger Paul Schurig missed the housewife in the home just as keenly as my father and I did. The house missed the housewife, and I missed my mother. But in the fledgling years a boy does not admit a thing like that, even to himself. He would sooner bite off his tongue.

The school holidays were still reserved for me. Nothing could change that. Sometimes Miss Dora with her high-piled hair joined us. But the great days of the walking tours into Bohemia and the wild pillow-fights at night in some country inn were gone for ever. The Golden Age gave way to the Silver Age, but that too had its glories.

My mother was now forty years old, and in those days a person was quite a lot older at forty than today. People remain young longer today and they live longer. And people grow taller. The progress of the human race is apparently taking the form of length. It must be admitted that this is an exceedingly one-sided growth, as may be daily observed. The longest reservoir, the longest plane journey, the longest life, the longest Christmas cake, the longest shopping street, the longest artificial thread, the longest film, and the longest conference – in time it overstrains even the longest patience.

My mother grew older and our hiking tours grew shorter. We confined ourselves to day excursions, but they too offered a wealth of beauty, and joy in abundance. In whichever direction we took the tram and at whatever terminus we got out, whether in Pillnitz or Weinböhla, in Hainsberg or Weissig, in Klotzsche or the Plauenschen Grund, we always found ourselves in the depths of the country and in the midst of delights. In half an hour one was as deep in the country as if one had been travelling for days. Wehlen, Königstein, Kipsdorf, Langebrück, Rosswein, Gottleuba, Tharandt, Freiberg, Meissen – wherever one alighted it was a holiday. The seven-league boots were no fairy-tale.

True, we had to use our own boots as soon as we come out of one of the little stations. But we had studied walking at the source. We knew how to step out. While other trippers groaned and perspired, we walked easily. And I now carried the bigger of the two rucksacks. It just happened that way, and my mother was glad.

Aunt Lina dipped deeply and energetically into her purse for the summer holidays of 1914 and sent both of us to the Baltic Coast with Dora. This was my first big journey, and for the first time I carried two suitcases instead of my rucksack. I cannot say that I was particularly pleased with the change. I cannot stand carrying suitcases. They give me the awful feeling that my arms are getting longer. And what would I want longer arms for? They are long enough, and even as a boy I never wanted them longer.

Changing from Anhalt to Stettin Station we treated ourselves to a horse-cab of 'second quality', and peering out between the luggage I got my first glimpse of Berlin. And the corn and clover fields of Mecklenburg were my first sight of a countryside without hills and mountains. The horizon was as level as if drawn with a ruler. The landscape was like a flat green board dotted with cows. I should not have cared to go hiking there.

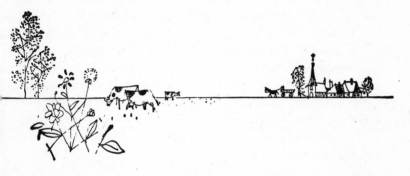

Rostock, with its harbour full of steamers, boats, masts, docks and cranes, pleased me better. And when we had to walk from a station called Rövershagen through a dark green wood where deer and roe, and once actually a pair of wild boar with their lively spotted young ones, darted to and fro across the road, I was reconciled to the lowlands of North Germany. I saw juniper trees for the first time in that wood, and I had no suitcases weighing down my arms. A carter had taken them and was to deliver them at Hoff's the fisherman's in Müritz East in the evening. The wind which was rocking the tree-tops already smelled and tasted of the sea. The world was different from the familiar world at home, but it was just as beautiful in its way.

An hour later I was standing among the sandhills, scratched by the coarse grass and looking out at that endless radiant mirror of bottle-green and many-hued blues and silvers – a breathtaking sight. At first my eyes were too startled to comprehend it, and then my comprehension was tinged with awe so that tears dimmed my first sight of that endless eyeless expanse. The sea was vast and blind, uncanny and full of mysteries. Wrecked ships lay on the sea-bed and dead sailors with seaweed in their hair. Down there, too, lay the sunken city of Vineta through whose streets mermaids swam, looking into the hat- and shoe-shops, although they wore no hats and certainly did not need shoes. Far away on the horizon a curl of smoke appeared, then a funnel, and now at last the ship; for of course the earth was round, and so was the sea. The waves with their white lace borders broke monotonously on the beach. They spat out shimmering jelly-fish which turned to pale aspic on the sand, and they washed up showers of murmuring shells, and pieces of golden-yellow amber in which flies and midges of past ages lay entombed, as in glass coffins, minute witnesses of the primeval world.

They were sold as souvenirs in the kiosk near the jetty, among the plums, children's spades and buckets, rubber balls, raffia hats and yesterday's newspapers. Here, on the fringe of the sublime, a ridiculous situation had developed. People had fled from the

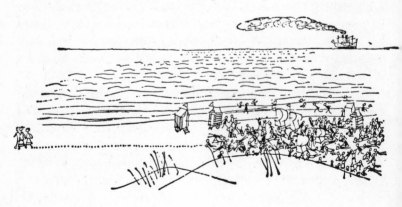

towns and now, faced with the infinite ocean, they were herding even closer together than in Hamburg, Dresden or Berlin. They huddled together in one little corner of the beach, noisy and sweating, packed as tightly as cattle in a truck. To left and right the beach was empty. The sandhills were deserted. The woods and the heathland were unfrequented. During the holiday season the tenements were on the seashore. They had no roofs; that was good. They had no doors; that was frightful. And the neighbours were brand-new; that meant revelling in brand-new contacts for the inquisitive. Humanity was sheep-like and flocked together.

We only went down to the beach to bathe and to walk along the jetty while the herd were in their lodging-houses taking their midday dinner or their supper. At other times we went for walks and trips as at home — along the coast towards Graal and Arend-see; into the woods past smouldering charcoal-piles; to lonely foresters' cottages where we were given milk and bilberries. We hired bicycles and rode through Rostock Heath to Warnemünde, where the human herds on the holiday pastures were far bigger than in Müritz. People baked in the sun in their thousands as if the herd were already slaughtered and lay in a vast frying-pan. Sometimes they turned over like voluntary cutlets. For more than a mile the air reeked of grilled humanity. So we turned our bicycles and rode back to the lonely heath. (Up here in Mecklenburg my mother had ventured on a bicycle again, for there were no hills by the Baltic. The unlucky back-pedalling brake was a superfluous gadget here.)

The world by the sea was at its most beautiful on clear, starlit nights. Over our heads many more stars than at home sparkled and twinkled, and they shone more magnificently here. The moonlight lay on the water like a silver carpet. The waves beat their eternal tempo on the strand. The intermittent rays of the Gjedser light flashed out at us — a greeting from Denmark, a country I did not yet know. We sat on the jetty in silence, over-whelmed by the mystery and unfamiliarity of it all. Suddenly we heard the distant sound of operetta music, coming slowly nearer. A coasting steamer, decorated with fairy-lights, was returning from one of the cheap popular 'Sea Voyages by Moonlight'. It lay alongside, rocking to and fro, at the head of the jetty, and a few dozen trippers came ashore. Chattering and laughing noisily, they hurried past our bench. Soon afterwards the laughter sank behind the dunes and we were alone once more with the sea, the moon and the stars.

On August 1st, 1914, in the midst of the joys of the holiday season, the German Emperor ordered general mobilization. Death donned his helmet. War seized the torch. The Four Horse-men of the Apocalypse led their steeds out of the stables. And Fate stepped with its jack-boots into the ant-heaps of Europe. The excursions by moonlight ceased, and no one stayed sitting in his deck-chair on the beach. Everyone packed up. Everyone wanted to get home. There was no holding them.

In the twinkling of an eye everything on wheels, down to the last cart, was hired, and so we had to walk through the wood, lugging our suitcases. This time no deer or wild boar scampered over the sandy roadway. They had all gone into hiding. With bag and baggage, lock, stock and barrel, the human stream rolled on. We were fleeing as if an earthquake had taken place behind us, and the wood looked like a green railway platform on which thousands of people were pushing and swarming with but one thought — to get away.

The train was crammed. All the trains were crammed. Berlin was like a witches' cauldron. The first reservists were marching to the barracks carrying flowers and paper cartons, waving and singing patriotic songs. Shouting newsboys were selling stop-press editions. The general mobilization order and the latest official announcements were pasted up at every street corner, and everyone was talking to everyone else. The ant-heap was in a state of wild upheaval and the police were trying to control it.

Special trains were standing ready in Anhalt Station, Berlin. We pushed my mother and the suitcases in through the window of a compartment and climbed in after her. On the way to Dresden we met troop trains full of soldiers who were being brought to the west. They waved toy balloons at us and sang, 'The Watch on the Rhine'. The fleeing holiday-makers waved to the soldiers, and Dora said, 'Father will sell more horses than ever now.' When we reached Dresden, sweating and exhausted, we arrived just in time to say goodbye to Paul Schurig. He too had to go into barracks.

The First World War had begun and my childhood was over.

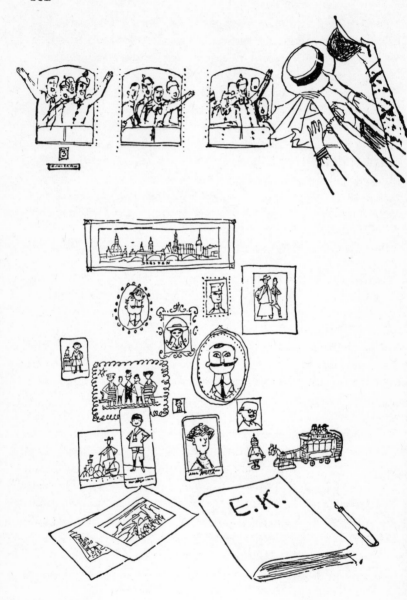

AND TO END – AN EPILOGUE

THE work is done. The book is finished. Whether I have succeeded or not, I cannot say. No one who has just written the
final page can know whether his plan has worked out well
or not. He is standing too close to the edifice which he has built;
he lacks the necessary distance. And he has no idea at all as to
whether his edifice of words will be good to live in, or not. I
wanted to tell how a little boy lived half a century ago, and I have
done so. I wanted to draw my childhood out of the domain of
memory into the light. When Orpheus took his Eurydice by the
hand in Hades he had orders not to look at her. Had I an order to
the reverse effect? Should I have looked only back and never
forward? I could not have done that, nor did I want to.

While I was sitting at the window writing my book the seasons
and the months passed through the garden. Sometimes they
tapped on the window-pane and I went out and conversed with
them. We talked about the weather. The seasons love that subject.
We talked about the snowdrops, and the late frost, the frozen
gooseberry bushes and the fragrant blossoming lilac, the roses and
the rain. There was always plenty to talk about.
Yesterday August tapped at the window. He was in a very
good humour, groused a bit about July as he does almost every

year, and seemed in a hurry. As he drew a little radish out of the ground he spattered my bean blossoms but said it was not his fault, and praised the dahlias and tomatoes. Then he bit heartily into his radish and spat it out again, for it was woody. 'Try another,' I said. But what do you think? He had already jumped over the fence and I only just heard him calling back, 'My kind regards to September, and tell him not to show me up.' 'I'll give him your message,' I called back. The months hurry by. The years hurry still more quickly. And the decades are in the greatest hurry of all. Only our memories have patience with us, especially if we have patience with them.

There are memories which we bury so well, like a treasure in wartime, that we ourselves can never find them again. And there are other memories which we always carry around with us like lucky coins. They have value only for us, and if we show them proudly and shyly to someone else, he will probably say, 'Goodness! An old penny! Why on earth do you keep a thing like that? Do you collect verdigris?' Many misunderstandings are possible between our memories and strange ears. I noticed that recently when I read a few chapters aloud to my four cats out on the terrace.

Anna, the youngest, who wears a black coat and white shirt-front, did not listen for long. She does not yet understand what is read aloud to her. She climbed up one of the ash trees and remained sitting in the fork, looking like a little head waiter trying to win some silly bet.

Pola, Butschi and Lollo listened more patiently to my reading. They purred several times. And they yawned several times, unfortunately without putting a paw to their mouths. Pola scratched herself behind the ear a few times. And when I had shut the manuscript a little nervously and laid it on the table, she said, 'You should leave out that about the wash-house, and the laundering and the mangling of the clothes at Ziesche the baker's.'

'Why?' I asked, and my voice sounded irritable. For my heart delights in the process which turns dirty clothes back into fresh, smooth, fragrant articles. How often had I helped my mother at almost every stage in this process! The clothes lines, the clothes pegs, the laundry basket, the sun and wind on the drying square at the coal merchant Wendt's in Scheunhof Strasse, the sprinkling of the sheets before they were rolled on the mangle, the squelching and draining of the gigantic mangle, the turning back and stopping of the wheel – was I to strike out all this white world of washing merely to please a black Angora cat?

'Pola is absolutely right,' said Butschi, the grey tom-cat who weighs fourteen pounds. 'Leave out the white washing. If you don't, we'll lie down on it and then you'll scold us.' 'Or you'll thrash us until your arm aches,' said Lollo, the Persian lady cat, scathingly. 'Do I thrash you until my arm aches?' I asked, indignantly. 'No,' replied Pola, 'but you're always threatening to do so, and that's just as bad.' 'Leave out the snow-white washing,' said Butschi, thumping the tiled terrace energetically with his tail. 'Otherwise there'll be trouble again,' declared Lollo, 'as there was recently about your beautiful white shirts. After all, it was not our fault that the linen-cupboard door was open and that it had rained outside.'

'Good heavens!' I cried. 'Surely there's a difference between real washing and washing in books. Real cats, however dirty they may be when they come in out of the rain, cannot lie down on written washing.' 'You're hair-splitting,' remarked Pola, beginning to wash her face. Lollo stared at me with her golden-yellow eyes, and said in a bored voice: 'You're a typical human being. Washing is washing, and thrashing is thrashing. You can't hoodwink us cats.'

Then all three stretched themselves and went off for a walk in the meadow. Butschi turned round once more and remarked: 'If only there were mice in your book. I even eat written ones. But you human beings are fine and careless. Not that that's anything new to us cats.' When half-way there he turned round again. 'I shall be a bit late home tonight,' he said. 'There's a full moon. Don't worry about me.' Now he too disappeared. Only the tall grasses, which moved above him, betrayed the direction in which he had gone. His best friend for the moment lives three doors away.

Well, I've struck out the laundry chapter, not for the cats' reasons, though they may be right. I had shown them one of my lucky coins, and now I stick it back in my pocket. I felt a little

sorry and a little offended, but after all there are vexations in every calling. To please the tom-cat I could easily bring in two or three mice instead of the washing, but I don't love my cats all that much! In the writing of reminiscences two rules are to be observed. One may, indeed must, leave out a great deal; and one must not add anything, not even a mouse.

Just now I sauntered through my meadow and stood for a while at the fence. Outside, the shepherd and his black collie were driving their flock of bleating sheep past. The little Easter lambs have turned into pretty big sheep after only a few months. With us human beings it takes longer. A little boy was standing by the roadside, looking at the sheep as they trotted along, and at the same time pulling up his stockings. Then he trotted along happily beside the sheep.

After twenty paces he stopped short because his stockings had come down again and he had to pull them up once more. I leaned inquisitively over the fence and looked after him. The sheep had got ahead of him and he wanted to catch up. Though they produce stockings, they don't wear any themselves, so possibly they are wiser than they look. Your stockings can't come down if you don't wear any.

The little boy stopped again near the market gardener's greenhouses. He pulled up his stockings, and this time he was desperate. Then he ran round the corner. I estimated that he must have got about as far as Gellert Strasse before they were down again. I've had lots of experience. Oh, those stockings! Oh, those memories! When I was a little boy my mother gave me elastic garters for my stockings, but they ...

Don't be alarmed, dear reader, I have finished. There won't be any stocking chapter, and there won't be any garter chapter. My task is done. The book is finished. Full stop. Where's the blotting-paper?